ON
PURPOSE

On Purpose:
Finding God's Voice in Your Passion

On Purpose
978-1-7910-2970-8
978-1-7910-2969-2 *eBook*

On Purpose: DVD
978-1-7910-2973-9

On Purpose: Leader Guide
978-1-7910-2971-5
978-1-7910-2972-2 *eBook*

Also by Magrey R. deVega
Questions Jesus Asked
The Bible Year
*Almost Christmas (*with Ingrid McIntyre,
April Casperson, & Matt Rawle)
Hope for Hard Times
Savior
Embracing the Uncertain
One Faithful Promise
Five Marks of a Methodist

Also by Jevon Caldwell-Gross
The Big Picture (with Nicole Caldwell-Gross)

Also by Susan Robb
Called
Seven Words
The Angels of Christmas
Remember (Coming December 2023)

Also by Sam McGlothlin
Advent: A Calendar of Devotions 2023

MAGREY R. DEVEGA, SAM MCGLOTHLIN, JEVON CALDWELL-GROSS, SUSAN ROBB

ON PURPOSE

Finding God's Voice in Your Passion

Abingdon Press | Nashville

On Purpose
Finding God's Voice in Your Passion

Library of Congress Control Number: 2023935971
978-1-7910-2970-8

MANUFACTURED IN THE
UNITED STATES OF AMERICA

CONTENTS

INTRODUCTION

Wouldn't it be great if we could hear God's voice? I mean to hear an actual, audible voice from God telling us what we are to do, who we are to be, and what we are to say. Let's admit that we are a bit jealous of some of our biblical ancestors. Apparently, they were able to hear God's voice, clear as day.

Like Abraham. He heard God say, "Pick up your family and move." And he did.

Like Moses. He heard God say in a burning bush, "Deliver my people." So, he did too.

Like Elijah. He heard God say in a still, small voice, "You're not alone." And he wasn't.

Wouldn't picking a job, selecting a mate, deciding on a house, even choosing what outfit to wear be a whole lot easier if we could hear God say to us, audibly,

"You should be a computer programmer. I like that for you."

Or, "That one, the brunette with the Bible and the nice family. Marry that person."

Or, "You don't look so good in green; wear the red with the matching pumps."

Wouldn't life be a whole lot simpler?

Unfortunately, as you've no doubt discovered many times over, life does not work like that.

The truth is the spiritual life is not as simple as picking up a red hotline phone to God. Instead, following Jesus is built on faith, and the practices that help us stretch, grow, and mature. In that way, learning *how* to listen for God's voice is just as important as what we hear God say. It is that regular flexing and developing of those spiritual muscles that help us grow in our faith and live life as God intends.

This is true especially when it comes to the biggest matter of discernment we face in our lives: not simply the clothes we choose to wear or where we choose to live or even the person we want to be with. When it comes to longing to hear God's voice, we are most hungry for a sense of purpose, direction, and calling in our lives.

That's as basic an ingredient to the human experience as they come. We want to be part of something bigger than ourselves. We want to participate in something that has eternal merit and lasting impact. We do not want to live a shallow, hollow existence. We yearn for deeper meaning, for deeper purpose within our lives. We want to be more than we are.

That is what this study is all about. *On Purpose: Finding God's Voice in Your Passion* is a four-part exploration of the spiritual principles that allow us to listen to God, discover our purpose and passion, join with others in the journey, and, ultimately, make a difference in the world around us.

- In Chapter 1, Jevon Caldwell-Gross will explore the barriers that prevent us from sensing the will and work of God in our lives.

- In Chapter 2, Magrey R. deVega will describe practical steps that will allow us to open our hearts and minds to God's voice.
- In Chapter 3, Sam McGlothlin will share how God is calling us through our own unique passions and interests.
- And in Chapter 4, Susan Robb will help us see how the task of hearing God's voice and discerning our purpose is best done in the context of community, in relationship with others on the journey.

By the end of this study, it is our prayer that you will be better at hearing God's voice and discovering the amazing purpose and passion that God is summoning of you. Together, we will learn to minimize the barriers that prevent us from listening to God and recalibrate our spiritual lives to be more in tune with who God is and how God is calling us. Ultimately, we will discover that listening together, in the context of community, will not only help us be part of something bigger than ourselves: God will use us to have an impact in the world far greater than the sum of our parts.

Welcome to the journey!

CHAPTER

1

Overcoming Obstacles

*Getting Ourselves
Aligned with God*

JEVON
CALDWELL-GROSS

Overcoming Obstacles

Getting Ourselves Aligned with God

JEVON CALDWELL-GROSS

Now the boy Samuel was serving the LORD under Eli. The LORD's word was rare at that time, and visions weren't widely known. One day Eli, whose eyes had grown so weak he was unable to see, was lying down in his room. God's lamp hadn't gone out yet, and Samuel was lying down in the LORD's temple, where God's chest was.

The LORD called to Samuel. "I'm here," he said.

Samuel hurried to Eli and said, "I'm here. You called me?"

"I didn't call you," Eli replied. "Go lie down." So he did.

Again the LORD called Samuel, so Samuel got up, went to Eli, and said, "I'm here. You called me?"

"I didn't call, my son," Eli replied. "Go and lie down."

*(Now Samuel didn't yet know the L*ORD*, and the L*ORD*'s word hadn't yet been revealed to him.)*

*A third time the L*ORD *called Samuel. He got up, went to Eli, and said, "I'm here. You called me?"*

*Then Eli realized that it was the L*ORD *who was calling the boy. So Eli said to Samuel, "Go and lie down. If he calls you, say, 'Speak, L*ORD*. Your servant is listening.'" So Samuel went and lay down where he'd been.*

*Then the L*ORD *came and stood there, calling just as before, "Samuel, Samuel!"*

Samuel said, "Speak. Your servant is listening."

1 Samuel 3:1-10

What did we do before GPS? (I got lost, a lot.) It's hard to imagine there was a time when we willingly traveled to unknown destinations with directions written on loose sheets of paper. *Make a right at the light. Go through three stop lights and make a left at the gas station. Once you pass the church with the stained glass windows and red door, keep going until there is a fork in the road. Make a left and then a sharp right.* I had as much trouble writing the directions correctly as I did following them. I am amazed I have not spent the last several years lost in a random city waiting for someone to rescue me from one of those wrong turns.

That's why I am certain that MapQuest was God's gift to the directionally challenged. The directions were detailed and included helpful information like street names and distances. One no longer had to depend on popular landmarks for directional cues. MapQuest's developers were even kind enough to allow the traveler to print out the directions with return routes automatically included. They knew people like me could not rely on simply reversing the original route. While it did not prohibit someone from missing a turn or miscalculating 0.3 miles, MapQuest made traveling a more enjoyable experience.

Then it all changed. GPS came along and made life even easier. The directional playing field was leveled. No more maps. Putting more paper into the printer just to find a nearby destination was no longer necessary. Frantically trying to find the written directions that fell to the floor when I knew the turn was quickly approaching was no longer a concern. With GPS, now there is a friendly voice that tells us exactly where to go. Just enter the address, and this voice takes over. It lets us know every turn one by one and reminds us when our exit is approaching on the left. The voice alerts us when there is "traffic ahead." The voice is protective enough to tell us there is an accident approaching and gives alternate routes to our preferred destination. I have depended on this voice to guide me to job interviews, kids' birthday parties, travel soccer games, and new restaurants for date nights. I don't know what I would do without it. I place my complete trust in this voice to guide me to where I need to be.

If only life were that simple. We all suffer from the effects of being directionally challenged at various points along our faith journey. We anxiously drive out into the unknown, praying to hear a voice. We arrive at the intersection of opportunities or big decisions and wonder which is the correct way. Should we follow the path on the left or the right? Where is God leading us? How do we live out our unique callings in this particular season of our lives? How do we use our gifts and passions as an expression of our faith and love for God?

Today, right now, is a critical time to have these conversations. It has always been an important topic within the church, and it's been emphasized a lot for the last fifteen years. But today's culture has added new demands and opportunities to the conversation. Most of us have more choices and greater opportunities than we might have expected even ten years ago. The internet and the expanded role of entrepreneurship has expanded the possibilities and potential spaces for people to embrace their passions. One no longer must depend on being hired by a particular company with a limited set of job openings. There isn't a need to have one's passions fit into a neatly defined box that's described by a job title. People have the power and opportunity to create their own spaces to live out their purpose.

If you don't believe me, log on to your favorite social media platform. People who have been gifted with immense talents in music, acting, or even writing no longer wait to be discovered. Those who feel a call to bring awareness to social justice issues and respond as social critics don't need tenure to do so. Now, they just press "send." Connoisseurs

We all suffer from the effects of being directionally challenged at various points along our faith journey.

in the kitchen can compile their favorite recipes into a self-published book and host their own YouTube channel where thousands will grow to trust their recommendations. The physical trainer who feels called to help people live and look like their best selves doesn't even have to meet you at the gym. The comedic personality doesn't need to wait for an agent. The preacher doesn't even need a pulpit. All it takes is a smart phone and the courage to expose one's gift to the world.

Let me be clear. You don't need the internet to live out your purpose. It's not generationally specific, nor is it available only to the tech savvy. However, it is a reminder of the many ways that people have creatively and courageously found ways to embrace their passions and live into their unique purposes. The internet has multiplied our choices and opportunities in a way that highlights the need for direction. Whether we find these opportunities in our jobs, in our hobbies, with a cause, within a community of faith, or even with our families, we all feel an innate pull to something more. As Magrey mentioned in the introduction, we desperately desire to have lives of meaning and purpose. We want to experience the joy and fulfillment that happens when we are connected to our passions. We want to know that our lives have made a difference. How do we discern the path God calls us toward, and how can we be sure we hear God's voice clearly?

Anyone who's ever felt this pull and needed guidance can attest to the difficulties and barriers that often stand as one anxiously waits for the next set of directions. Listening to

God's voice is an essential part of our journey of discovery, yet at times it almost seems impossible. We go to great lengths to hear God's voice. We fast. We pray. We give up things for Lent. We ask the advice of others hoping that maybe God will speak. The Bible makes it seem so easy! And yet, so often, we are met with silence or delayed responses. Sometimes the directions are clear, but the reasons are questionable. We know we're taking a left turn now but are unsure where we're headed in the long term. Then there are times when the destinations are obvious, but the paths from here to there are ambiguous or illogical. Where are the burning bushes or still small voices? Where is the divine GPS?

So, we begin our journey acknowledging the barriers that will be present as we desperately seek to hear from God. What stands in our way? What prevents us from hearing and discerning God's voice clearly, and how can we move past these obstacles? In my own life, and in helping others hear God's voice, these are the most common barriers I've discovered: lack of recognition, dead spots, difficulty of hearing heard things, and mistaken identity.

The story of the prophet Samuel helps us identify these barriers and how we might begin to overcome them. We look at them not through the lens of someone who had it all figured out but through the story of someone who heard God's voice and was utterly confused. While we admire those that clearly hear from God through burning bushes and mountaintop experiences, the majority of us have a story similar to that of Samuel.

Lack of Recognition

Samuel was the son of Elkanah and Hannah. He was literally an answer to a prayer. Unable to bear children, his mother, Hannah, found herself outside of the temple at Shiloh with tears in her eyes. As her spiritual exhaustion and frustration reached a breaking point, she prayed for God to give her a son. She made a vow that if the Lord answered her prayer, she would give this son over in service to God. The Lord heard Hannah that day, and she delivered a son and named him Samuel, which means "God has heard." She remembered the vow that she made. When Samuel was of age, Hannah gave him over to be raised mentored, and trained by the priest Eli.

Samuel spent the next few years learning under the tutelage of Eli. He lay down one night and heard a voice calling his name. Thinking it Eli, he went to the priest to await further instructions. Eli said he didn't call Samuel. The voice Samuel heard did not belong to the old priest. It was not a voice that Samuel could distinguish.

Samuel's initial barrier was his inability to recognize God's voice. He heard God but was unsure of who was speaking. This almost seems out of place considering Samuel spent most of his time in the temple working for God. He was not unaware or ignorant of religious practices. However, when the opportunity presented itself, he could not differentiate God's voice from the other voices in his life, especially the voice of his mentor, Eli.

The lack of recognition is a familiar barrier. It's a test of our ability not just to hear what's been communicated but to determine whether this is God's prompting or something (or someone) else. We ask ourselves, "How do I know if this is God's voice?" As we search for clarity in purpose and spaces that fuel our passions, there will always be several competing voices and messages. We have the voices of culture continuously speaking to us about where we find value and worth. We may have the voices of our friends and family offering their solicited and unsolicited opinions about what they feel is best for us. We even have our own inner dialogue that can be both our worst critique and our biggest supporter. How do we recognize God's voice amid all these others?

Recognition assumes a certain level of familiarity. However, familiarity is built over time. It's not something that happens overnight. It takes time to learn what God's voice sounds like (or looks like or feels like).

If God spoke in only one way, this might have made it easier for Samuel. It might have expedited the learning. But God has been known to speak through clouds, fire, rain, floods, plagues, famines, men, women, music, miracles, and blinding light—just to name a few! That night, God spoke to Samuel through an audible voice that sounded at least somewhat like Eli. There are an infinite number of ways God gets our attention. It takes time to develop this skill of recognizing when and how God speaks to us. Listening requires learning. Learning requires patience.

It takes time to learn what God's voice sounds like (or looks like or feels like).

I learned this as a sophomore at Kalamazoo College when I enrolled in the class The History of Jazz. Our professor was determined to train our ears. Regardless of our musical backgrounds, he wanted to help us become better listeners. He would play songs from Louis Armstrong, Miles Davis, John Coltrane, Duke Ellington, Ella Fitzgerald, Dizzy Gillespie, Billie Holiday, and others. After hearing a song once, our professor would ask us to listen closely so we could hear underneath the music. First, we had to learn the different styles and sounds of the various musicians. Then, we had to identify the different instruments being played in the songs. He would shout over the music, "Do you hear a tenor or alto sax? What's keeping the beat and rhythm of this song?" He encouraged us to just listen because according to our professor, listening was a learning process.

The first barrier to hearing God's voice is our inability to recognize it. The way to overcome this barrier is to learn, over time, what God's voice sounds like. We train ourselves to listen to God's voice and recognize when it speaks. It takes a willingness to keep laying down until we get the clarity we need or the competency is developed. No one just gets handed the keys to a car as a teenager and immediately drives across the country. We take tests. We log a certain number of hours behind the wheel under the supervision of a parent or guardian. We practice until we are comfortable to drive on our own. Think of the many other things we have been required to learn. We've had to learn how to speak, walk, count, and even forgive. Some of us have experienced learning how to teach, how to parent a child, how to love a spouse, or even how to connect through a screen. We learn to use new apps on a phone. We didn't come into church knowing all the songs and hymns, but we learned them over time. We learn new things about people. We learn new things about ourselves. What now seems so basic was at once a new skill that we needed to acquire. We tried. We failed. We learned. Life is a constant invitation to learn. The same is true for hearing and recognizing God's voice.

We place so much pressure on ourselves to get it right the first time. We get frustrated when we have to lie down again and again. But remember, Samuel didn't understand or comprehend the events the first time around. Let that sink in. He needed to be patient with the process, and he needed to be patient with himself. He needed helpful guidance from Eli about what to say. So be kind to yourself. Give yourself time. Finding clarity and understanding God's purpose for your life is going to require more than one conversation. Sometimes, you will get it wrong. (Read that as many times as you need.) There will be moments when you leave more confused than when you started. Be patient with yourself. It's a journey of failures.

It takes time to learn how to decipher God's voice from the many other competing voices in your life. It's a skill that is developed through trial and error. We try. We fail. We try again. But if we are patient, if we are willing to keep trying and continue learning, eventually we start recognizing the voice on the other end. If God is patient with us, we need to offer the same grace to ourselves and to the process of discerning and even listening. So go back and lie down again and again—however long it takes for you to hear and recognize God's voice.

Dead Spots

I am currently the Teaching and Online Campus Pastor at St. Luke's United Methodist Church, located in Indianapolis. The sanctuary that holds our traditional worship is breathtaking. It has a seating capacity of over 1,500 people and when full, the energy in the room is contagious. I often find myself standing in the sanctuary staring at the stained glass cross or admiring the enormity of the pipe organs.

With all the accoutrements of such a space, I was shocked one day to hear complaints about the sound! It's happened several times since. Every so often, a concerned member will remind us they have difficulty hearing the voices speaking from the pulpit. After spending thousands of dollars on sound engineers, we learned there were certain "dead spots" in the worship space. Because of the sanctuary's acoustics, one could have a slightly different audible experience depending on where one decided to sit. Certain spots in the room are dead spots, where it can be harder to hear. It's not easy telling a member who has sat in a certain space as part of their Sunday morning routine that they have chosen to sit in a place where the sound doesn't travel well.

You don't have to travel to Indianapolis to experience the complexity of acoustics. Does it ever feel like you are in a spiritual dead spot—a place where it's hard to hear from God? Our faith journeys will undoubtedly include seasons or situations when hearing from God becomes difficult. God graciously speaks into our lives, but we fail to fully grasp what's being said. We earnestly pray, but the verbal exchange is not reciprocated. We check the lines of communication and realize that maybe the problem is not with the sender. Maybe we are not in a good place to hear from God. Here are two common dead spots that make it difficult for God's voice to be amplified in our lives.

Distractions

Have you ever noticed that when you are looking for an address while driving, you naturally turn down the music in your car? In order to focus on the task of finding a particular destination, we naturally remove the distractions or conflicting stimuli to help us focus. We get rid of things that might compete for our attention. Hearing from God can be difficult when we are surrounded by distractions.

We live in a culture that prides itself on productivity and the perception of busyness. From the moment our day begins, we are bombarded with to-do lists, social media notifications, and emails that need our responses. Some people have kids to get off to school or morning commutes to work. Perhaps our homes have now become our offices. By the middle of the day, the notifications and emails have already increased. By the end of the day, dinner needs to be cooked. Bills need to be paid. The emails keep coming. Someone needs to start the bedtime routines. Dogs need to be walked. Clothes need to be washed and folded. There will never be a shortage of things vying for our attention.

In his call narrative, Samuel was invited to go back to sleep so that he could hear from God. God spoke when he was lying down. When he rose, thinking Eli called him, Eli told him three times to go back to sleep. God spoke to Samuel at night, in the quiet, in a space free from the things vying for his attention so that he could give God his full attention. While the ideal space looks different for many people, the outcome is the same. We can move out of a dead spot by intentionally removing or reprioritizing certain aspects of our lives so that we can we give God the attention that God deserves. It's an invitation and challenge to quiet the many other voices around us. It's faithfully and courageously turning the volume down on all of the noise around us so we can better search for our destinations—and hear God's voice telling us the way.

Disobedience

The beginning of 1 Samuel 3 reminds us that, "The LORD's word was rare at that time." There were not many recorded divine visitations or notable revelations. This was not an indication of God's inability to speak but of the community's inability to listen. This was one of many periods in the history of Israel when they failed to obey God's commands and expectations. God spoke to Samuel near the end of the time of the judges when Israel wavered between obedience and disobedience. They set their own standards. They had a desire to live like the nations around them.

We can move out
of a dead spot
by intentionally
removing or
reprioritizing
certain aspects of
our lives so that
we can we give
God the attention
that God deserves.

To put it plainly, there are times we don't hear from God because we don't want to. We place ourselves in a dead spot of our own making. We intentionally turn away from the very places God is trying to lead us. We hear the instructions but tune God out because we decide we know a better way. The Bible refers to this as being a stubborn people (Exodus 32:9; 33:3; Nehemiah 9:16). My mother calls it being "hardheaded!" It's what characterized the people throughout the Book of Judges, as the Israelites repeatedly turned away from God to follow their own way. The Israelites at the beginning of 1 Samuel had failed to see that the less they listened, the less God spoke.

This is what made Samuel unique. In a period where the word was rare, Samuel heard God calling his name. It wasn't his experience that made him stand out. It wasn't the influence that he amassed over the years. He was different simply because he was willing to obey when God was directing his purpose. We often think of faith as our willingness to trust God. Obedience reveals how much God can trust us. Obedience is a discipline of showing God that we not only hear with our ears but also with our actions. Obeying God's voice amplifies the space. It creates an environment where the acoustics create more opportunities for sound. The more we listen, the more God speaks.

Difficulty of Hearing Hard Things

When Samuel hears God call his name again, I admire his response: "Speak. Your servant is listening." There is an openness to this reply. Samuel has absolutely no knowledge of what God is going to say or where God is going to lead him. However, he's willing to listen. His ears and heart are receptive to what God has to say. He is not coming with preconceived ideas or expectations. His listening is not conditioned by what he already wants to hear. He is simply open. And that is enough.

Such openness is often unfamiliar in our search for clarity in purpose. Our hearing is normally filtered through what we might call *always already listening*. It's a way to describe the act of listening that is already preset to certain messages. We listen for the outcome that always confirms what we already believe to be true. We listen for certain hoped-for messages or tune out or downplay answers that might cause us to rethink things. Another way to say this is, we hear only what we want to hear. We hear before God even speaks. We have the answer determined before God even offers the choice of paths. We approach God with a mirage of openness that is masked with our own agendas. Our openness has its filters. Our receptivity has its limits. Our response sounds like this: "Speak Lord, for your servant is *always already* listening."

This posture of listening reminds me of Colonel Jessup's infamous statement in the movie *A Few Good Men*. Jessup, played by Jack Nicholson, sits on the witness stand being questioned by the charismatic lawyer Lt. Kafee, played by Tom Cruise. Kafee is trying to uncover truth behind the murder of a marine by two fellow marines. In a heated exchange, Lt. Kafee demands the truth. Colonel Jessup, noticeably upset and offended, shouts, "You can't handle the truth!"

Listening with openness requires that we be willing to hear the truth—even a truth that might be hard to handle. We stay open because eventually, living with purpose invites us to hear hard things. There is often a gap between what we want to hear and what God says. The message we hear from God will undoubtedly stretch our faith. It might demand aspects of ourselves or our gifts that we didn't know were possible. We mistakenly come with our preset messages only to find that the words, leading, and directions are often hard to hear.

As Samuel made himself available to hear from God, he heard these words:

> *The LORD said to Samuel, "I am about to do something in Israel that will make the ears of all who hear it tingle! On that day, I will bring to pass against Eli everything I said about his household—every last bit of it! I told him that I would punish his family forever because of the wrongdoing he knew about— how his sons were cursing God, but he wouldn't stop them. Because of that I swore about Eli's household that his family's wrongdoing will never be reconciled by sacrifice or by offering."*
> *(1 Samuel 3:11-14)*

Surely this can't be the very first message Samuel receives from God! So much for being open! I don't imagine that's what he wanted or expected to hear. The message was hard: it pronounced punishment on Samuel's mentor, Eli. How could Samuel approach the person that has done so much for him with a message of doom and gloom? Can you imagine the inner dialogue that Samuel had with himself? Can you feel his palms sweating as he thinks about relaying this message?

God could have started with a message far more inspirational and hopeful. God could have reminded Samuel of the important role he would play in the history of Israel. God could have told him he would be a prophet or that he would anoint Saul and David as the first kings of Israel. Yet in this first message there was no mention of prophets or kings. There was no conversation around the impact he would have on the entire nation. It was a powerful, unsettling message of judgment on Eli and his family.

We learn from Samuel's story and our own lives that God's voice and directing isn't always accompanied by pleasantries and comfortable commands. This is the challenge of listening. God often tells us things that we don't want to hear. It puts even the most faithful of us at an interesting crossroads. We want the voice to direct us, but only to the places that are comforting—lands flowing with milk and honey. We love to hear a barrage of good news and favorable odds. However, listening requires surrendering. It demands courage, asking that we put aside our preconceived expectations and abandon our preset stations. We are challenged and invited to stay open even to the things that are hard to hear.

This is critical as we listen for God's voice because God has a pattern of arriving with messages that are as challenging as they are inspirational. Are we open to hearing the hard things? God came to an elderly couple with a hopeful message that their descendants would be as numerous as the stars, but Abraham and Sarah would have to move to an unknown place and leave behind the life they had spent years building.

Listening requires surrendering. It demands courage, asking that we put aside our preconceived expectations and abandon our preset stations.

That same voice would visit an eighty-year-old man named Moses with a speech impediment who was trying to run from his past and challenge him to stand before Pharaoh and proclaim a message that would disrupt a nation. Jesus visited the shores of Galilee and invited a group of would-be disciples to abandon their previous places of safety and security.

As people throughout the Bible answered their calls and courageously embraced their purpose, it was often on the heels of hard conversations and difficult truths. Hearing from God challenged them, and it will undoubtedly challenge us. What we hear could move us from places of comfort and require us to do, say, and experience things that are far beyond our imagination. It will stretch us. It will demand certain aspects of our personalities and gifts we have yet to explore. It might require a level of boldness and courage that we once thought impossible. It will take us to places where it seems we are utterly lost. But on the other side of these things that can be difficult to hear, we can find meaning. We discover possibilities that we never dreamed to be available. We unearth passions and joys that seemed impossible.

Mistaken Identity

"What is God calling me to do?" It's a question that many people of faith continuously ask on their journey of discovery. It's asked by the person graduating with a diploma and by the person facing retirement. It's a question we ask when considering changing professions or making a move or before any other life-changing decision. We pray about it. We ask the opinions of others. Sometimes the question brings a certain level of excitement as it ushers in new adventures and opportunities. Most times, it's the cause of anxiety and frustration. We are prone to question the road ahead and even doubt the worth and the meaning of our previous experiences. Even so, we convince ourselves that answering the question of *what* will solve our problems and ease our anxieties. This can prevent us from hearing God's voice because we have a misaligned understanding of our identity, believing that *what we do* is the most important thing about *who we are.*

Underneath our search for *what* is a subtle assumption that our purpose is attached to a particular sets of tasks: a career, a position, a role. As a result, our identities are mistakenly tied to job titles and responsibilities that can be too easily taken away. We can't hear God's voice in our passions because we are starting with the wrong questions. We are looking to find the answers in positions that are temporal and many times unsustainable. Our previous beliefs about our worth and value are questioned when the availability of these activities is threatened. Circumstances like COVID-19 push us to look for purpose beyond our level of productivity. This can either force us into dark places of despair or invite us to redefine and reshape where we find purpose.

When God gets the attention of Samuel, God does not bombard Samuel with a list of responsibilities or have an in-depth conversation about Samuel's calling. Instead, three times, God simply calls Samuel's name. At the time, a child's name often served as an affirmation of what the parents or community believed about the potential and possibilities of that child. A name was more than just a noun. Names were attached to a purpose. Samuel's name came with a meaning. *Samuel* means "God hears." His name carried with him a story of God's provision. His name was a reminder of a miracle. The calling of his name was reminder that Samuel was an answer to a prayer. It easy to gloss over this aspect of his call narrative, but it's the foundation. God affirms who he is before he tells him what to do.

With every call of Samuel's name, God affirms that Samuel is a child of God. Before Samuel would be called to anoint the future kings of Israel or encourage them in battle, he was reminded that was an answer to a prayer. Samuel had a list of titles, including prophet, priest, and judge. Sometimes the assignments changed and the titles became blurred, but his identity remained. Through them all, he was Samuel. One of the most important questions that we must continually ask ourselves is, Who am I? Who is God calling you to be? That question is foundational to what God is calling you do. As we seek to discover God's voice in our passions and purpose, let us not forget that *who we are* is more important than *what we do*.

I was reminded of this a few years ago after an incident we had with one of our children. It's helpful to know that before our kids go to sleep, my wife or I have a routine we do with them called "head to toes." After they shower, brush their teeth and are completely ready for bed, we recite an affirmation that goes like this: Joshua, I love you from your

As we seek to discover God's voice in our passions and purpose, let us not forget that **who we are is** more important than **what we do.**

head to your toes, from your fingertips to your nose. Joshua, Daddy loves all of you because you are a gift from God."

I must admit, early in their childhood it didn't appear as though they were paying much attention during this routine. They laughed, squirmed, asked to use the bathroom, reminded us they forgot their favorite stuffed animal downstairs. We clearly enjoyed this more than they did. Most nights it felt like these words were falling on hard soil.

That was until my wife was taking our oldest son, Joshua, into the dance studio and a gentleman clearly battling mental illness spat on him and called him a name offensive to African Americans. It shook all of us, especially my son. It was hard explaining to a five-year-old why this happened. It was the first time he asked what the "N-word" meant. We didn't have the luxury of shielding our child from the harsh realities of our world. As he gathered the meaning and asked questions for further understanding, I thought his little spirit would be broken. I thought I'd have to spend days, months, maybe even years undoing the damage that was done. Until he responded, "That man must not have known that I'm a gift from God."

We can learn a lot from five-year-olds. In that moment it didn't matter what he did or what he wanted to do when he got older. That wasn't important to him. He found an identity that could not be taken away by anything external. It's a reminder that who we are is so much more important than what we do. Our identity is not tied to a job description but to the reality that we are gifts created by God. For most of us, the *what* will constantly change. We will be called to do different things in various seasons of our lives. Our passions may change and evolve. Jobs will change. Titles will come and go. Listening to God's voice is an invitation to be reminded of who we are, not just the things we are called to do. It may take years to embrace, but as we search for a life of greater purpose and clarity, it's a great place to start.

Are there barriers to hearing God's voice? Absolutely. Finding God's voice in our passions may require more than just passively listening for a voice off in the distance. This journey will require the equivalent of handwritten directions, paying attention to how God is speaking, looking for certain signs. It will mean reading scripture, praying, learning, listening, remaining open, and knowing when to turn off the radio and remove all distractions. It will mean listening to hard things, things we might think at first that we can't handle. And yet we trust that if that voice has gotten us this far, it will continue to lead us to a place of meaning and purpose even if it's sometimes hard to believe in the moment. Buckle up and enjoy the journey.

Questions for Reflection and Discussion

1. Which barriers do you often find are the most difficult to overcome as your listen for God's voice?

2. What are the unique ways that God speaks to you? Are there spaces that you revisit to help amplify God's voice?

3. Why do you think we place more emphasis on the task we are given versus the people we are called to become?

4. What things or responsibilities have you attached to your identity and purpose?

CHAPTER
2

Raising
Awareness

Practical Steps for Hearing God's Voice

MAGREY R. deVEGA

CHAPTER 2

Raising Awareness

Practical Steps for Hearing God's Voice

Magrey R. deVega

My son, accept my words
and store up my commands.
Turn your ear toward wisdom,
and stretch your mind toward understanding.
Call out for insight,
and cry aloud for understanding.
Seek it like silver;
search for it like hidden treasure.
Then you will understand the fear of the Lord,
and discover the knowledge of God.
The Lord gives wisdom;
from his mouth come knowledge and understanding.

He reserves ability for those with integrity.
    He is a shield for those who live a blameless life.
He protects the paths of justice
    and guards the way of those who are loyal to him.
Then you will understand righteousness and justice,
    as well as integrity, every good course.
Wisdom will enter your mind,
    and knowledge will fill you with delight.
Discretion will guard you;
    understanding will protect you.

                                        Proverbs 2:1-11

My son, don't forget my instruction.
    Let your heart guard my commands,
    because they will help you live a long time
    and provide you with well-being.
Don't let loyalty and faithfulness leave you.
    Bind them on your neck;
    write them on the tablet of your heart.
Then you will find favor and approval
    in the eyes of God and humanity.
Trust in the Lord with all your heart;
    don't rely on your own intelligence.
Know him in all your paths,
    and he will keep your ways straight.

                                        Proverbs 3:1-6

We long to hear God's voice. We want to live with meaning and purpose, and we trust in God as the ultimate higher purpose for our lives, the one place in which meaning and fulfillment can be truly found. But as we saw in chapter 1—and as you likely know all too well from your own experience—most of the time God doesn't speak with a clear, audible voice, giving us step-by-step, turn-by-turn navigation. Sometimes there are barriers in our way, which prevent us from sensing God's presence and finding our purpose. Naming and surrendering those barriers, as Jevon Caldwell-Gross showed us in chapter 1, is an important step. But what comes after that?

In this chapter, we'll explore some practical ways to listen for God's voice and discern God's will for our lives. That's not to say there is a set formula to follow that guarantees the Holy Spirit will speak clearly. Nor is it to say that God's communication lines are restricted only to these things. What I want to suggest is that God often chooses to speak through these means, and that by practicing them we open ourselves up to God's presence, training our eyes and ears to recognize where God meets us and where God would lead us. And it all starts with the same idea: listening for God's voice and living into God's future means moving forward, one step at a time.

Stepping Backward into the Future?

A few years ago, my older daughter, Grace, asked me, "Dad, if you had a time machine, would you choose to go back to the past or skip ahead to the future?"

It was such a simple question. I was surprised at how hard it was to answer.

Would I go back to my past to relive those things I have already known about, with all its highs and lows? Or would I jump ahead into some time down the road with no guarantee that the future would be better or worse than now, or what the journey was like to get there? I wonder how you would answer that question.

In William MacAskill's book *What We Owe the Future*, he says that every culture on earth thinks about the future as being in front of us and the past as being behind us. Every culture, that is, except one. The Aymara, an indigenous people in Bolivia and Peru, think about the future as behind them, and the past as being in front of them. When they think about an event in the past, they point *ahead*. When they think about a possibility in the future, they point their thumbs *behind their back*.

How does that make sense to them? Because they recognize that the past is the only thing they can see with clarity. That is not the case with the future. We don't have eyes on the back of our heads, and we can't see the future clearly. The Aymara would say that in a way, all of us are walking backwards into the future.[1]

This is all to say that when it comes to being stuck in the past or trying to predict the future, the best way to live—perhaps the only way to live—is to focus on the present moment, which is the only thing we can know for sure.

The first way to open yourself to God's voice is to focus on the here and now.

That's where the Book of Proverbs comes in, along with the other Wisdom Literature books of Job, Psalms, Ecclesiastes, and Song of Solomon. They don't focus on the past, like the history books of Kings and Chronicles before them. Nor do they talk about the future, like many portions

The first way
to open yourself
to God's voice is
to focus on the
here and now.

of the prophets after them. Instead, we learn from Proverbs the value of focusing on the present moment, and moving into the unknown of the future, just one step at a time.

It is a point captured most succinctly and most famously in Proverbs 3:5-6, which calls us to trust in the Lord with all our hearts, to not lean on our own understanding, but in all our ways acknowledge God, and God will direct our paths. When it comes to hearing God's voice and discovering God's purposes for us, we should only worry about the next faithful step that God has given us to take and not worry about steps two or three or ten—or the final outcome—until God has revealed the next step to take. This is what it means to not lean on our own understanding: we take the next step, in God's pace, in God's time.

Living this way is not easy, as you well know. We want to know what the future holds. But as the Aymara people have recognized, we cannot see what lies ahead.

That's when faith steps in to give us the courage and confidence to move even though we cannot see the final destination. Author Phillip Yancey once put it this way: "Faith means believing in advance what will only make sense in reverse."[2] When we are facing what feels like an impossible situation or a very difficult decision or whatever is making the future so daunting, the best way to strengthen our faith and lean not unto our own understanding is to take things one faithful, trusting step at a time.

When I think about times when I have had to remind myself to trust in God one step at a time, I have often thought about that iconic scene in the third Indiana Jones movie,

Indiana Jones and the Last Crusade. Indy is in search of the legendary holy grail, the cup used by Jesus in the last supper. After entering a cave, he comes to the edge of a cliff, with a wide, deep chasm separating him from the other side. He realizes that the distance is too great for him to jump, and he says out loud, "It's a leap of faith."

Behind him, Indy's father realizes it too. Struggling from an injury, the older Doctor Jones says, "You must believe, boy. You must believe." Then, with the suspenseful crescendo of John Williams's famous musical score, Indiana picks up his foot, leans out over the cliff, and steps forward. He finds himself landing on an invisible stone bridge, midair, which was only illuminated when he was courageous enough to take the next step in front of him even though all he could see was emptiness. When it comes to hearing God's voice and discovering our purpose, believing is seeing.

What that means is that we don't control the timing of when the next step will be revealed. But it is in those moments of waiting, in those in-between steps, that the most important work of faith occurs. Our faith is not just demonstrated in the courage to take the next step when it's time. Our faith is stretched in between the steps, when we wait, trusting that we are where God has called us, unsure even of when the next step will be revealed, much less what direction it will lead us.

Not long ago I saw a picture on social media of a sign in front of the First Baptist Church in Newton Centre, Massachusetts. It's a large banner with a series of letters jammed together that reads two different ways, depending on how you see it:

GODISNOWHERE

One could read it as, "God Is Now Here" or as "God Is Nowhere." Those are two very different ideas. When I first saw the picture, I thought, "Wow. Whoever is in charge of signage at that church just blew it." But then I realized the deeper, more profound point.

Where and how you observe the space in your life determines when and how you notice God's presence.

The space in your life matters, just as it does in that church sign. Those moments in between the steps of our journey are not a time for panic, nor are they a time to passively do nothing, nor are they a time to pursue distractions and diversions. The in-between spaces are a time of faith building, of watching, praying, discerning, and trusting. They are a time to look for confirmation that the path you're on continues to be the one God wants for you. Or to look for holy speed bumps that indicate that God's timing is a little slower than you expected or wanted. Or to look for detour signs that show that God wants to nudge you in a slightly different direction than you were thinking. Or to simply pull over and rest for a moment, to clear your mind and heart so that God can silence all voices except for God's voice.

Then, and only then, God will show you the next step, when you are called to take it. This is what it means to live by faith, one step at a time.

Faith in the In-Between Times

Back in 2018, my father was diagnosed with cancer of the bladder. It was a surprising diagnosis, given that there is not a lot of history of cancer on my father's side of the family.

After a series of tests and meetings with oncologists, my father had a difficult decision to make about the course of treatment he would follow. My mother, two brothers, and I knew that the ultimate decision was his and that we would honor whatever treatment path he sensed was best for himself.

In that "in-between" time, between diagnosis and next step, I had a candid conversation with him, in which he said to me, "Magrey, I'm ready for my faith to be tested." It was a beautiful and amazing thing to hear. In addition to weighing the pros and cons of the different treatment options, and in addition to processing all the information from the doctors, he was using his in-between space to fortify his faith. My father knew that even when the next step was revealed, there would be more steps to take after that. Rather than worry about what those steps might be, or where this would ultimately lead, he just wanted to make sure his faith was strong, that his ability to discern God's spirit was clear, and that he was taking moments to breathe and not worry about the things he could not control.

Now, four years later, my dad is on the other side of his cancer treatment. He tackles new health challenges as they come, just as he has throughout his life. One doctor's visit at a time. One test and result at a time. One ache and pain at a

41

time. One gifted day and breath and beautiful moment with family at a time. His faith has been tested. And he is learning to walk backwards into the future, sight unseen, one faithful step at a time.

I think about my dad not just because of his remarkable faith during his battle with cancer, but because in 1978, when I was five years old, he gave me my first Bible as a Christmas present. It's a brown, bonded leather, King James Bible that he purchased by redeeming S&H Green Stamps in St. Petersburg. When he came home and gave it to me, I opened it to notice that he had written an inscription just for me.

It reads: "Dearest Magrey, May you make His Words in this Holy Book your guide in life from this day and hereon!" And then, at the bottom, he wrote the words to Proverbs 3:5-6 (KJV):

> *Trust in the LORD with all thine heart; and lean not unto thine own understanding.*
>
> *In all thy ways acknowledge him, and he shall direct thy paths. And he signed it, "Daddy."*

The first principle in hearing God's voice and discovering God's purpose involves taking things one step at a time, including being faithful in those moments between the steps. That's what it means to trust in the Lord, with all your heart.

Scripture

Another practical principle in opening yourself to God's voice can be summarized by a simple acronym. It is "S.O.S."

The first principle in hearing God's voice and discovering God's purpose involves taking things one step at a time, including being faithful in those moments between the steps.

You may recognize that as the same acronym for the iconic distress signal, "Save Our Ship." In this context, it means something else. S.O.S. is a simple way to remember three means God often uses to speak to us: Scripture, Others, and Silence. We see throughout the Bible, Christian tradition, and our own prior experiences, that God often chooses to speak to individuals in these ways. By spending time regularly reading scripture, listening for the voice of God's spirit through others, and by spending time along with God in silence, you can open yourself to God's voice. Scripture, Others, Silence.

First, consult the Scriptures. That ought to be no surprise. For thousands of years, people have gained comfort and guidance from the Bible, from ordinary people like you and me to even historic, iconic figures like Queen Elizabeth II, who said, "To what greater inspiration and counsel can we turn than to the imperishable truth to be found in this treasure house, the Bible?"[3]

Elizabeth certainly had difficulties throughout her long, illustrious life, like in 2002, when both her sister and her mother died. Later that year, in her Christmas message to the Commonwealth, she shared how she turned to her faith for daily strength. She said, "I know just how much I rely on my own faith to guide me through the good times and the bad. Each day is a new beginning. I know that the only way to live my life is to try to do what is right, to take the long view, to give of my best in all that the day brings, and to put my trust in God."[4]

The Bible gives us the guidance to take each day as a new beginning, to take the long view, and to offer God our very best. Discovering that for yourself involves reading the Bible daily to develop the spiritual muscle memory to make it an integral part of your life. There are many programs and reading plans for spending time in the Bible every day. One such program I would recommend is *The Bible Year: A Journey through Scripture in 365 Days*. For a whole year, you will read the entire Bible, cover to cover, guided by a daily devotional. It would be even better to do it with a small group of people with whom you can share insights and discover profound meaning.

But we also know that there are those unique, singular moments when we turn to the Bible in specific moments of challenge praying for a timely insight of wisdom, comfort, or strength.

So, to help you in those kinds of moments, the back of this book contains a listing of over eighty Bible passages that you can turn to when you are experiencing different kinds of challenges or adversity in your life (pages 127-132). Are you feeling fearful? Or helpless? Are you concerned about the state of the world, or trying to repair a broken relationship? How about feeling busy, or just trying to be a good parent? This list specifies twenty-one different kinds of challenges you might be facing, and for each one, gives you four different scriptures that you can look up that might help you.

45

Others

The second part of S.O.S. is Others. It is the principle that, when we are seeking to hear God's voice in times of distress, we can best hear it in the company and companionship of other people. You will explore this idea more fully with Susan Robb in chapter 4, but for now we can name the benefit of having trusted people by your side when you need help. I turn to select clergy friends who are in my covenant group, or my therapist whom I see regularly, or members of my family. I hope that you have those kinds of people as well.

I would also offer you an intriguing bit of guidance from the Quakers. They have developed a practice called the Clearness Committee, but you don't have to be a Quaker to use it. A Clearness Committee works like this. If you are the one seeking to hear God's voice, then you assemble a group of family and friends whom you trust. What is unique about this time together is that the others in the room are not there to give you advice or to tell you what to do. They are there to simply listen and to ask you questions. These are not leading questions that indicate what they think you should do. Nor are they questions that stir argument or debate. The Clearness Committee asks simple, gentle questions that prompt your own ability to listen to your inner awareness of God's voice. I have known a number of people who have used a Clearness Committee to help them discern matters of vocation, family, and life.

There are numerous resources available on the internet in case you want to learn more, including those offered by an author named Parker Palmer, who has popularized the idea of a Quaker Clearness Committee.[5]

Silence

The final part of S.O.S. is Silence. All throughout the Bible, we read of people who heard the voice of God only after they were able to silence all other voices, including their own. Elijah heard the still, small voice of God on Mt. Horeb, only after he stopped listening to his own preconceived expectations of God (1 Kings 19:11-13). Zechariah accepted the promise of God for him and his wife Elizabeth only after a nine-month period of silence (Luke 1:19-20, 63-79). Jesus escaped the noise of life often throughout his ministry, including in the wilderness before his ministry began (Mark 1:12-13; Matthew 4:1-11; Luke 4:1-13). One of my favorite prayers that I offer in my own spiritual life is simply, "God, silence all voices but your own."

It's amazing what silence can do to bring you clarity. In his marvelous book *Creativity: A Short and Cheerful Guide* (Crown, 2020), the great comedian John Cleese suggests that moments of inspiration, creativity, and wisdom can come only after we push the pause button on our conscious mind and let our subconscious do its work. In other words, after we have done all sorts of noodling, mental crunching, and thinking about a problem with the information processing part of our brain, it is often best to disengage from a problem so that the

It is often best to disengage from a problem so that the true genius of our brain, the subconscious, can begin to toss around all that data and give us a spark of insight.

true genius of our brain, the subconscious, can begin to toss around all that data and give us a spark of insight. It's why some of our best aha moments come when we are exercising, showering, washing dishes, or taking a walk. We'll explore this idea further in the next section of this chapter.

Let the acronym S.O.S. guide you in hearing God's voice and discovering God's purpose for your life. Even when times are hard, or God's voice seems quiet or absent, stay faithful in these spiritual practices during these in-between times. Consult the Scriptures. Lean into the wisdom and gentle companionship of others. Embrace silence to quiet your mind.

Listening with Our Subconscious

The final practical principle we will explore is the notion of whether and how God speaks through our subconscious. To put it more directly in the form of a question: Does God speak through our dreams?

For starters, consider these famous works by some notable artists: The song "Yesterday" by The Beatles. Salvador Dali's painting *The Persistence of Memory*. The blockbuster film *Inception* by director Christopher Nolan. The poetry of Edgar Allan Poe.

What do you suppose all these iconic works have in common? Well, the idea for each of these masterpieces came to the artist in a dream. The songwriter, the painter, the director, and the author all received the ideas for their creations while dreaming. Also consider the numerous instances of biblical figures who received divine instruction or inspiration in the middle of their dreams: Jacob, Daniel, Ezekiel, Peter, John, and others.

Consider your own dreams. When we dream something, to what degree is it that God is speaking? How can we be sure? Does God speak to us today in our dreams, just as God spoke to people in their sleep in the Bible?

Edgar Allan Poe was pretty clear in his own mind about the answer. This is what he said:

> That dreams, or, as they were then generally called, visions, were a means of supernatural instruction, if we believe the bible at all, is proved by Jacob's dream, the several visions of Ezekiel and other prophets, as also of later date, the Revelations to Saint John; and there appears no reason why this mode of divine communication should be discontinued in the present day.[6]

So, what if Edgar Allen Poe is right?

Now, rest assured, I'm not going to explore this idea through some esoteric perspective, or with astrology or New Age spirituality. Nor am I interested in telling you exactly what your specific dreams might mean for you.

Making such a promise would be like a story from one Valentine's Day morning when a woman woke up and said to her husband, "Honey, I just had the most amazing dream. I wonder what it means. I dreamt that you gave me a diamond necklace later today as a Valentine's Day gift. What do you think that dream means? on Valentine's Day?" (Wink, wink.)

The husband smiled and said, knowingly. "Huh. I think you'll know tonight."

Sure enough, later that night over Valentine's Day dinner, the husband handed her a gift. She opened it, and it was a book titled, *The Meaning of Dreams.*

So rather than try to interpret what your particular dream might mean, here is some insight into why we dream and what God might be saying to you.

Why We Dream

A few years ago, the *Journal of Neuroscience* published a study by the University of Rome that concluded that dreaming is the brain's way of dealing with unresolved emotional attachment to certain memories from our past. In other words, you and I have had things happen to us that have strong emotions attached to them. Sometimes it's worry and anxiety related to trauma. Sometimes it's grief related to loss. Sometimes it's longing, anger, or bitterness related to a broken relationship.

Dreams, the study suggested, help us process emotions. When we've been unable to find a healthy way to address heavy emotions—like talking to a friend or therapist or finding resolution with the other person in that relationship—then those unresolved emotions might surface in our dreams.

Why? It is our brain's way of sorting through the unresolved emotional strain and thereby releasing us from the potentially hazardous side effects of repressing those emotions, which could otherwise surface as heart trouble, high blood pressure, and other physiological stresses.[7]

So this might be one way that God is speaking to you through certain dreams. What heavy emotions are you carrying from which God wants you to find a healthy release? What will you do to process and release those feelings rather than bottle them up? Jesus said that we should release our burdens to him because his yoke is easy and his burden is light.

Dreaming might be one indicator of what exactly those burdens are.

Gaining Insight and Creativity

It is also possible that God wants to use our dreams to speak some new insight or nugget of inspiration or creativity to us. Harvard Medical School did a study in which a professor had her students focus on a problem to solve, and then told them to go to sleep. What they found was that it is possible to come up with novel solutions to those problems in their dreams. In fact, two-thirds of those participants had dreams that addressed their chosen problem, while one-third actually came up with solutions in their dreams.

Here are some famous examples: Jack Nicklaus had been laboring over his golf game when in the middle of a dream he thought about a different way to hold his golf club. His swing improved after that.

Billy Joel, Beethoven, and The Beatles all supposedly heard new melodies and new arrangements in their dreams, which they promptly used to inspire new music.

The inventor of the sewing machine, Elias Howe, had struggled in 1884 to figure out how the needle could work in a

Jesus said that we should release our burdens to him because his yoke is easy and his burden is light.

machine for sewing. In a dream, he found himself surrounded by indigenous people with spears that had a hole in the point. When he woke up, he realized that a needle with a hole in the point would solve his problem.

And then there's me. While I do not claim to be in the league with those people, I depend on the power of dreams myself to help me do what I do every Sunday morning. In order to preach a sermon week after week, I have developed a writing routine that I stick to regularly. I have a deadline to have my sermon written by noon every Wednesday. I then film it for the online service on Thursday mornings and get the manuscript to the roughly fifteen staff and lay people who need my sermon by noon on Thursday so they can fulfill their various responsibilities such as planning worship.

It all starts with writing the sermon on Wednesday by noon. So, every week, I follow the same routine. On Wednesdays I get up at 6:30 in the morning, and out the door by 7:00 to some local coffee shop or restaurant. There I read through the scripture text, pray, ponder, and read a few favorite sources for biblical insight and inspiration.

Then I'm home by 8:30 a.m., and I spend the next ninety minutes crunching things in my head. I think about the key parts of the text, make connections, brainstorm examples, and turn over words and phrases in my mind. I have not yet written a single word on the screen, but I am mentally gathering all the relevant bits and pieces, angles and interpretations, and possible directions the sermon will go.

By 10:00 a.m., I am exhausted. I am usually still searching for that one little hook, the key point, the pivot, the aha, the memorable thing that the rest of the sermon will be built around. The sermon isn't finished yet; it isn't really started, but the key idea is almost there. And my brain is tired.

So that's when, I am unashamed to say, I take a nap. Right in the middle of sermon writing. From 10:00 a.m. to roughly 10:20, I close my eyes and sleep. Twenty minutes. When I wake up, I usually have the last bit of inspiration I need to bring the sermon home.

I used to feel weird about doing this. But do you know what? It works for me. And I'm not the only one.

Forbes magazine published an article about how the sweet spot for that kind of "inspiration napping" is right before you drift into light sleep and long before you fall into deep sleep. Thomas Edison often took such naps in his chair holding a bunch of marbles in his hand so that at that moment as he was just falling into light sleep, he would awaken to the sound of marbles hitting the floor. That would often be the moment when his subconscious kicked in with just the right insight on whatever invention he was working on.[8]

So, back to my Wednesday morning nap time. After I wake up from twenty minutes of barely drifting off, most of the time, I have it. That little nugget of clarity comes to mind, and I can finally begin to see the entire structure of the sermon: main points, key stories, the opening ninety seconds, and most importantly, the transitions between them all. I believe that insight comes from God in my sleep.

And it will usually then take me only seventy-five minutes to write the sermon by my noon deadline.

On Sundays, when I am actually delivering a sermon live and I see someone falling asleep while I preach, I chuckle to myself. They are falling asleep to a sermon that I fell asleep writing.

So, can God speak to you in a dream? I think it's possible. Sometimes God can use dreams to help you name unresolved emotional hardship that you need to work through in a healthy way. Sometimes God can use dreams to give you inspiration and insight. And yes, God can sometimes speak to you a word of direction and guidance that you are seeking in your life.

Of course, interpreting what that message is requires discernment and companionship. Use S.O.S.—Scripture, Others, and Silence, especially the first two letters. Check your interpretation against a faithful reading of scripture, and the counsel of wise friends, and the moral values and Christian teachings of the church. Check it against what your prayer life, your gut, and your life experience might be saying to you. God speaks to us in a number of ways, often simultaneously, and never in contradiction with the other messages God is sending. Open yourself to God's leading, God's speaking, and God's direction, with confidence and trust. Whatever God is saying to you in your dreams can and will be verified in the other ways God is speaking to you.

This chapter has offered a handful of practical approaches you can follow to hear God's voice and discover God's purposes in your life. Take things one step at a time and pay attention to the in-between moments. Practice S.O.S.,

God speaks to us in a number of ways, often simultaneously, and never in contradiction with the other messages God is sending.

reading the Scriptures, listening with Others, and practicing Silence. And pay attention to the ways that God might be speaking through your subconscious, always checking those messages against the other ways God is speaking to you.

This is not a comprehensive list. God can and will speak in many ways besides these. You might find yourself resonating with some of them more than others, depending on your situation and your experience. But know that throughout the Bible and Christian history, God often has spoken to others in these ways. Open yourself to God's voice and direction, the leading of the Holy Spirit, however it comes. God is always speaking to us, and we have ways to listen, trust, and follow God faithfully into the future.

Questions for Reflection and Discussion

1. When has it been difficult for you to listen for God's voice one step at a time? Even when it was hard to do so, what were the benefits?

2. How will you begin to apply the principles of Scriptures, Others, and Silence in your spiritual practices?

3. When do you think God has spoken to you in your dreams?

CHAPTER
3

Channeling Our Passions

*Discovering
Our Gifts and
Making a Difference*

SAM MCGLOTHLIN

Channeling Our Passions

Discovering Our Gifts and Making a Difference

SAM McGLOTHLIN

When everyone was being baptized, Jesus also was baptized. While he was praying, heaven was opened and the Holy Spirit came down on him in bodily form like a dove. And there was a voice from heaven: "You are my Son, whom I dearly love; in you I find happiness."

Luke 3:21-22

It was supposed to be a warm, beautiful spring weekend. Instead, it was rainy and cold. Our family and friends had traveled across the Southeast to witness our wedding. It began with our rehearsal dinner, housed at an inn that sits on top of Monteagle Mountain in Tennessee.

I remember the room was cozy, bringing warmth the weather did not deliver. I was sitting at a long table with my closest family members. In the center, there were green vases of all shapes and sizes cradling bright, bold April flowers. There were candles sitting in bird cages, thin cuts of steak, clear glasses of wine, people eager to uphold my partner Mark and me as we claimed one another through the vows of marriage.

As is customary, my soon-to-be father-in-law, John, stood up to welcome our guests and say a prayer. He said the typical phrases people expect: "Thank you for traveling here. We are so glad Mark met Samantha. We are thrilled she will be a part of our family."

Then there was a pause. It was long enough that my diverted eyes quickly made their way back to his face. As I searched it, I realized he was pausing because he had gotten choked up. In a room full of people, there he stood trying to hold back tears.

I'll never forget that moment: someone getting choked up over me. He wasn't just saying routine words. He meant them. They made me feel affirmed, loved, and claimed. It was a parental blessing, the kind that makes you feel capable of anything. It was the kind of blessing that launches you forward because you know who has got your back.

When we talk about finding our purpose and our calling, we must first begin with the understanding that we are affirmed, loved, and claimed by God, doused with a parental blessing that launches us forward in life.

We see this happen at the baptism of Jesus. In Luke chapter 3, we are told that John (the Baptist, not my father-in-law) was baptizing people in the wilderness. He was telling them to come to the water and repent of their sins. But he also told them that someone else was coming, someone who would baptize them with the Holy Spirit.

We do not receive many details in Luke as to what happened when Jesus approached the water. We are told only that, "When everyone was being baptized, Jesus also was baptized."

Why was he baptized? None of the Gospels tell us exactly why. Here is my theory: Jesus was baptized to prove he really did come to be one of us. He came to receive the affirmation and love of his Father. In the water—the same water the rest of us are baptized in—Jesus too received the Holy Spirit. He came as we do to claim his purpose and calling.

As Jesus was praying, heaven opened, and the Holy Spirit came down on him in bodily form like a dove. A voice from heaven said: "You are my Son, whom I dearly love; in you I find happiness."

Matthew records a slight difference. In Matthew, instead of "*You are* my Son, whom I dearly love; in *you* I find happiness," we hear the voice say: "*This* is my beloved Son, in whom I am well pleased" (Matthew 3:17).

Because of the nuance between the two, some scholars suggest that in Matthew, the crowds could hear the affirmation, but in Luke, it was just for Jesus.

I'm glad the Gospels give us both versions. We need both. Isn't it true that sometimes it is more empowering when others hear someone claim and affirm us (like how I felt when my father-in-law, John, publicly expressed gratitude for me)? And at other times, we just need to hear it for ourselves. We need to hear God whisper in our own ear, in our own soul: "You are mine. I love you. I claim you."

This is Jesus's starting place. And it is our starting place because in baptism we enter the same water. We are loved, affirmed, and claimed by God.

What I am saying is: God gets choked up over you.

If that blessing is our beginning, if we know God has our back, then we are capable of anything.

What we also see in this text is that during his baptism, Jesus received the Holy Spirit: the One who commissions and calls.

This Spirit of God would serve as his counselor, comforter, and course corrector, much like the Spirit would do when it descended on the disciples in the absence of Jesus-in-the-flesh (Acts 2).

I wonder if this is why Luke says the Spirit descended on him in "bodily form." It came as a dove, but I wonder if Luke is also hinting at the nearness of the Spirit for Jesus going forward. This Spirit must have been so tangible that Jesus could touch and taste it; it must have been God in his belly and in his bones.

That proximity to God is precisely the point. When we are given the Holy Spirit that lives and dwells in us, we make

We are loved, affirmed, and claimed by God....If we know God has our back, then we are capable of anything.

a home for God in our very being. God becomes a guide from the inside, so much a part of us that we are never without God's wisdom and prompting. It is the Holy Spirit within us that leads, drives, and sends us. It is the Holy Spirit that commissions and calls us.

We know this because after Jesus is baptized, Luke chapter 4 tells us that he is driven, sent, led into the wilderness by the Spirit. The Spirit is the One who sends.

But sent to do what? That is what we are trying to figure out. Sent for what purpose?

We see that Jesus is sent into the wilderness to be tested and tempted for forty days before he begins his ministry. I wonder if this time in the wilderness afforded Jesus space to learn what he was made of, to practice rejecting the evil powers of this world and renouncing the spiritual forces of wickedness. Perhaps his wilderness was an incubator for what was to come in his life, a warm-up for how he would eventually resist the evil, injustice, and oppression of the Roman empire and the very reality of sin and death.

Why would I say that? Let's take a look at Luke 4:14-19. It says:

> *Jesus returned in the power of the Spirit to Galilee, and news about him spread throughout the whole countryside. He taught in their synagogues and was praised by everyone.*

> *Jesus went to Nazareth, where he had been raised. On the Sabbath he went to the synagogue as he normally did and stood up to read. The synagogue assistant gave him the scroll from the prophet Isaiah. He unrolled the scroll and found the place where it was written:*

The Spirit of the Lord is upon me,
  because the Lord has anointed me.
He has sent me to preach good news to the poor,
    to proclaim release to the prisoners
    and recovery of sight to the blind,
    to liberate the oppressed,
    and to proclaim the year of the Lord's favor.

Then Jesus rolled up the scroll and said, "Today, this scripture has been fulfilled just as you heard it" (Luke 4:21). In other words, I am the One this prophecy describes. This is what I was sent by the Spirit to do.

I believe the same is true for us. If Jesus is claimed, commissioned, and called to preach good news, proclaim freedom, recover sight, liberate the oppressed, and proclaim the year of forgiveness, then as his followers we are sent to do the same. We are baptized as Jesus was. We receive the same Spirit that sent Jesus. It is by the same power of the Spirit that we are able to reject the evil powers of this world and renounce the spiritual forces of wickedness, seeking freedom and justice for all people.

If that is the case, then *how* we do it is where our unique gifts, interests, and passions come in. We do that first by paying attention for the divine nudges or prompts in our lives that meet us right where we are.

Divine Deliveries

I am huge fan of the Netflix series *Manifest*. If you haven't seen it, I am about to ruin it for you. It's about passengers on

Montego Air flight 828 who disappear while traveling from Jamaica to New York City, only to reappear five and a half years later. Some of the main characters are Michaela Stone, a NYPD detective; her brother, Ben Stone, a college associate professor in mathematics; and Cal Stone, Ben's young son, who is dying from cancer.

Miraculously, when the passengers land safely and return home, they have not aged at all. Meanwhile their loved ones in New York City have started living different lives in light of their perceived deaths. As the series unfolds, we see how their disappearance gives many of the passengers a second chance. For example, Cal returns to find cancer treatments advanced enough to save him. Michaela is able to help people after working through the agonizing guilt she carried from a pre-flight car accident that killed her best friend.

But the biggest surprise and real premise of the series is that flight 828 passengers start receiving messages, hearing voices, and feeling nudges. Over time, the passengers begin to refer to these promptings as "callings." At times the callings are so loud they cannot ignore them. At times the callings are cryptic, and they have to put all the puzzle pieces together to solve them. At times there isn't a voice or a feeling but a drawing or picture or melody to follow.

We see the passengers love-hate relationship with the callings. We see the destruction and missed opportunities that happen when they don't follow the callings. We see their pain and frustration when a calling is hard or unclear. Yet overall, the passengers believe that the callings are divine deliveries.

They come to regard the callings as promptings that lead to saving people, bringing more hope, healing, and wholeness to the world.

I think this is how the Spirit of God operates. God's spirit sends us messages, nudges us, gives us feelings in our guts that we just know we are supposed to follow. (The God in our belly and in our bones.)

The more we listen, the more clearly God's messages come through. We might miss opportunities. We might become frustrated when callings are unclear, or we might have to be patient as we follow a large volume of nudges before all the puzzle pieces come together. But God is always speaking, always prompting. We just have to pay attention. When we do, we discover our particular callings, the way God prompts us through the power of the Holy Spirit, just as the spirit led Jesus.

Let me add that I know it can sound intimidating and unobtainable to think about pursuing the same kind of calling Jesus did: preaching good news, proclaiming freedom to prisoners, recovery of sight to the blind, liberating the oppressed, and announcing the year of forgiveness.

Perhaps for some of us, we are meant to take that commission and call literally as it is written. For some of us— perhaps for you—it is meant to be expanded in our literal, lived experiences. There are literal prisoners that need our attention and companionship. And there are people shackled and stuck in their shame who need to hear the grace and love of Jesus Christ. But remember: good news, freedom, recovery,

God is always speaking, always prompting. We just have to pay attention.

liberation, and forgiveness can be delivered in myriad ways. Often it is those nudges and callings from God that lead us simply to become divine mail men and women. Those messages send us to offer a friend an encouraging word, to help someone free their mind from rumination, to provide a meal for someone having a hard week, to sing a song that seeps with freedom, to say, "I am sorry, let's work through this."

In other words, callings happen to us and around us every day. These nudges can add up to our capital-C Calling. Or they can stand alone as our way to daily deliver the goodness of God's kingdom. There is no right or wrong, and they are not mutually exclusive. Both capital-C Callings and everyday callings (daily deliveries) lead to saving people, to bringing more hope, healing, and wholeness to the world.

What We Know and Love

God often speaks to us through the things we know and love. At the beginning of a new year, many churches follow the journey of three magi who made their way to worship Jesus. We don't really know if there were three of them, but we presume so because there were three gifts: frankincense, gold, and myrrh. What we do know is they were Gentiles. They were not waiting on a savior or messiah. They were people who studied the sky, likely Persian men from a priestly class known for dream interpretation and their knowledge of the stars.

At the time, it was common practice for astrologers to watch the sky, as most people believed the stars offered signs that could be interpreted to foretell the future or decide on a course of action in the present. One idea was that stellar phenomena often accompanied the birth of an important or extraordinary person. As these men, the magi, were doing what they knew, loved, and were trained to do, they saw something that glimmered in their eyes. Matthew 2 tells us they made their way to Herod and asked: "Where is the newborn king of the Jews? We've seen his star in the east, and we've come to honor him."

Now, this terrified Herod because he was the king. He wanted the glory, power, and honor. So Herod called the chief priests and the scribes together to ask what the scriptures say, and they quoted Micah 5:2, which says the shepherd of Israel will come out of Bethlehem.

So Herod called the wise men to him in secret, told them to go and search for the child and bring back word of his whereabouts so that he could also worship him. The magi set out on a journey not knowing where they were going but trusting the star in the sky to lead them. Upon coming to the house, they saw Jesus and Mary. We are told they bowed down and worshipped Jesus. Then they opened their treasures and presented him with gifts of frankincense, gold, and myrrh.

Something about Jesus must have captivated and compelled them because we also hear that they defied Herod by not returning to him. Having been warned in a dream— which they were experts at interpreting—they went home a different way. We might easily imagine that after worshipping Jesus, they went home as different people.

I love starting every new year off with this story for two main reasons.

First, these men were Gentiles. They did not practice Judaism and did not worship God as the Jews did. And yet, God used what they knew and loved to speak to them. The fact that it was a star is an added bonus. God can be found in the serenity of the stars and the flickering glow of firelight. When we talk about finding God's voice in our passion, here it is.

God uses what we know and love to speak to us, to beckon us toward Jesus. We don't even have to be in a state of expectation for a Savior. Even in our unbelief, God reaches out to us and gives us signs to trust and follow.

What do you know? What do you love? How could those gifts, interests, and passions be used to glorify God?

The second reason is this: when the magi arrive, we are told they bow down and worship Jesus, placing their gifts at that tiny child's feet. This posture of surrender, of worship, cannot be overstated as we search for God's voice in our passions.

The spiritual life requires practice. We have to practice laying our hopes, dreams, worries, and fears before God. Over and over, we have to present our gifts, interests, and passions to Jesus. It is in that space of surrender that we become more available to God. We stop striving and contriving. We stop denying and defying. As we bow down and worship Jesus, we find ourselves so captivated and so compelled that we want to go about life a different way, as different people.

The spiritual life requires practice. We have to practice laying our hopes, dreams, worries, and fears before God.

Repurposed for the Kingdom

Speaking of what we know and love, further on in Matthew chapter 4, we come across two brothers, Simon and Andrew. They are fishermen, people who know the best and worst spots on the Sea of Galilee to get a catch. As they are doing their work, Jesus walks along the shoreline and calls out to them. "Come, follow me," he said, "and I'll show you how to fish for people" (Matthew 4:19). Then we are told they quickly drop their nets and follow him.

These two men are the first disciples Jesus calls in Matthew, Mark, and Luke. The readiness and ease with which they leave their occupation and families has always baffled me. I wonder if those impulsive yeses were followed by long talks with their wives.

We are not so quick to drop everything and follow Jesus, especially not our livelihoods or our families. I wonder then if this image is meant to be a metaphor, less literal and more lesson. Or hyperbole, an exaggeration to make a point. Or the irony of the gospel: you have to give up everything in order to find everything.

These fishermen who drop their nets and leave their families and follow Jesus are just the first disciples to get it. A widow will drop two copper coins in the temple treasury as the rich pour money in. Jesus will acknowledge that she is the one who gives it all up. A woman named Mary will drop to the feet of Jesus at a dinner party, pour out an expensive perfume with a strong fragrance that fills the room, and anoint Jesus for death.

Throughout his ministry, Jesus will say things like: "All who want to come after me must say no to themselves, take up their cross, and follow me. All who want to save their lives will lose them. But all who lose their lives because of me will find them" (Matthew 16:24–25).

The puzzling prescription of the Christian life is that losing leads to finding. The holiest of equations is that subtraction equals addition. Laying oneself and one's life before God as an offering leads to greater fulfillment, passion, purpose, and abundance.

The good news after we give it all up is that Jesus holds on to what we know and love and repurposes it for the Kingdom. We don't really lose everything, it is just redirected. Jesus's tutelage, his on-the-job training, takes us from fishers of fish to fishers of people. Our gifts, interests, and passions cast a wider net than they once did, and we learn the best and worst spots to get a catch. God speaks to us in what we know and love, and we surrender these gifts of ours to Jesus. It is in that intersection of calling and surrender that our passions lead to God-given meaning and purpose.

I met Harold when I was first appointed to Belle Meade United Methodist Church in Nashville, Tennessee, seven years ago. He was standing in the back of our early worship service, running the slides that were projected onto the screen. I soon learned that he was a whiz when it came to tech stuff (his occupation) and was always volunteering his time to help us out with computers in the administrative office.

When the pandemic hit, he was one of the first non-staff members incorporated back into the worship services on Sundays. Like most congregations, we started virtual ministry we wished we had implemented much earlier before it was a necessity. Harold helped to run the live stream on Sundays. His gifts were invaluable.

Over the years, I have witnessed how incredibly selfless Harold is. He is hardly ever seen or acknowledged as he sits in the Land of Oz (what we call our AV room) making sure our worship services stream on Facebook and YouTube. He makes in-kind purchases or gives donations that he doesn't want anyone to know about. He hops on a phone call or comes to church at any hour to troubleshoot an issue, all while expecting nothing in return. He shows up every single week with a smile on his face, excited to serve, thrilled to be a part of what God is doing through our church.

Harold is someone who knows what it means to surrender your gifts, interests, and passions to Jesus so that they are repurposed for the Kingdom. What Harold is good at, Jesus uses to reach hundreds of people every Sunday.

You can be in the background or in the limelight. You can be a financial analyst or a baker, a soother of children or an "I'll do anything" volunteer. Whatever you are good at, Jesus can use. Lay it all in his hands and see what he does with it. Drop your nets and follow him.

Rhyme Time

Sometimes we struggle with naming what we are good at. We know the surface-level skills and abilities we possess, but we need others to reflect the deeper stuff back to us. As Magrey mentioned in chapter 2, one way to approach finding our gifts is to speak with others, to listen for what others call out in us.

Most mornings, I take my son, Lewis, and my daughter, Madeline, to work with me. They attend the children's center that is a ministry of our church and a stone's throw away from my office. Ever since Lewis learned the "rhyme time game" in his preschool class, he wants me to feed him a word so he can name one that rhymes. So, this is what we do in the car: "Tree. Knee." "Green. Mean." "Road. Toad." And my favorite: "Pickle. Tickle." Each correct rhyme must be accompanied with, "Ding! Ding! Ding!' And each incorrect rhyme with "Whomp. Whomp." You can imagine how he fights with me over correct and incorrect rhymes.

Sometimes I make it more challenging for him by asking him to think of a third or fourth word that rhymes with the initial one. Sometimes he says a correct word but doesn't know what it means, so I ask him to define it. (By the way, it is surprisingly hard to explain what "lurch" means to a four-year-old.)

Truthfully, I am impressed with what he comes up with. One morning I told him, "You're so good at this, buddy." He said, "I know, Mom." Later that evening, without my prompting, he remembered what I said and brought it up to his dad. "You know I am really good at the rhyme time game." It mattered that his mom called it out. It gave him confidence and affirmation.

If this sounds familiar, it's because it is another way to think about what we saw earlier, about being claimed. At times, we are empowered when others hear someone claim and affirm us. At times, we just need to hear the voice of God speaking directly to our souls. At times, we need those in our lives to call out what we are good at in a way that gives us confidence and affirmation.

In the faith community, we miss opportunities to expand a disciple's learning and help them find what they are excited about when we do not cultivate and call out their gifts. It makes me think of Paul's words in 1 Corinthians 12:1: "Brothers and sisters, I don't want you to be ignorant about spiritual gifts." Part of our role as the body of Christ with many parts is to inform one another of our gifts. There are different gifts but the same Spirit, the same Lord, the same God at work in each of us.

So what can we start calling out and naming in one another? How can we help one another find our Kingdom Callings?

In other words: it's always the right time to deliver a good rhyme. (Cheesy, but you know you laughed.)

What Brings You to Life?

When I was nineteen years old, I went to work for a nonprofit ministry in rural Appalachia called Mountain T.O.P. (Tennessee Outreach Project). During high school, I had been to camp for one week at a time every summer with my youth group. Mountain T.O.P. is where I discovered that

In the faith community, we miss opportunities to expand a disciple's learning and help them find what they are excited about when we do not cultivate and call out their gifts.

faith and action go together. It is where I learned that God could be found in the serenity of the stars and the flickering glow of firelight.

As a college summer staffer, I became responsible for those youth and adults who came to camp to partner with families through Mountain T.O.P. Their workday consisted of minor home repair projects, and their evenings brought dining hall dance-offs, silly games, and worship filled with wonder. This meant I had to haul wood in an old pickup truck and pretend to know how much of it was needed to build a porch, and I was responsible for planning and leading worship.

The first night I stood up to give the message, I was trembling. The community of at least five hundred people (okay, it was one hundred, but if felt like five hundred) were seated on old railroad ties in front of three wooden crosses. It was dark enough that I had to use a flashlight to see my notes. I had written them on a coveted Flippy—one of those small notepads held together with silver spirals. There is no way I could tell you what I talked about. It was as if I left my body and flew above everyone, while at the same time I felt the hot blush of red on my face while speaking.

Afterward, I was walking back to the girls' cabins to sing them a song and turn out their lights. An adult whose face I could not pick out of a lineup came up to me and simply said, "That was brave." And even though I can't remember what exactly he was referencing, this stranger in the dark was the first to fan the flame of something that was ignited in me that night.

What I discovered was that preaching brought me to life. I was scared, but my heart raced with excitement and my spirit soared when I spoke. I later learned the words of Jeremiah 20:9, "But there's an intense fire in my heart, / trapped in my bones. / I'm drained trying to contain it; / I'm unable to do it." That was how I felt.

That moment sent me on a path to discovering my capital-C Calling. It led me to see the way I could proclaim freedom, recover sight, liberate the oppressed, and announce forgiveness.

So let me ask you: What brings you to life?

Does your heart race and your spirit soar when you do it? Do you feel like you are exactly where you need to be?

If the answer is yes, then I think you too, have found your capital-C Calling—the big thing you can't imagine yourself not doing even if the context or details morph over time.

If the answer is no, then perhaps it is time to test the waters and try something new. Maybe you just haven't discovered what it is that brings you to life.

God wants you to find that flame and fan it. God wants you to feel that fire in your bones.

Bind Up the Brokenhearted

In the Book of Matthew, after Jesus is baptized (claimed, commissioned, and called) and after he calls the fishermen, he begins his ministry in a threefold manner: teaching, preaching, and healing. Teaching, preaching, and healing are how Jesus lives out what the Spirit has commissioned him to do; it is how he lives into his call to bring good news, freedom, recovery, liberation, and forgiveness to the world.

This means that another way to couch our quest for how our gifts, interests, and passions can be used for Kingdom purposes is to ask: How can I teach, preach, or heal?

I am particularly drawn to Jesus's healing ministry, which included words but also tangible, tactile, God-in-the-flesh touch. Jesus touched children who were dying. He touched women who were bleeding, men ravaged by demons, and lepers pushed to the outskirts of the city. Jesus touched those who were sick with fever and those who were paralyzed and forced to beg for money. Jesus noticed and healed them all. Jesus was affected by their suffering and extended to them the grace of a healing touch.

If you look closely at Isaiah 61, the scroll Jesus unrolled and read in the synagogue in Luke 4, you see special attention on healing. It says: "He has sent me…to bind up the brokenhearted…/ to provide for Zion's mourners, to give them a crown in place of ashes, oil of joy in place of mourning, a mantle of praise in place of discouragement" (v. 1, 3). Healing may have just been the biggest part of Jesus's call.

An older mentor and friend of mine likes to ask: What breaks your heart? If we can find what breaks our heart and do something about it, then people hanging on to the fragments of their beings have companions in gluing the shards back together. We help bring joy in the midst of mourning. We share shouts of praise that replace despondent discouragement.

The need for healing will always be present.... That is one focus, one mission, one vision every part of the body shares—one calling that will never change.

In our world, the need for healing will always be present. People will always be hungry for good news, freedom, recovery, liberation, forgiveness, and a balm for their wounds. That is one focus, one mission, one vision every part of the body shares—one calling that will never change.

What brings you to life? What do you know and love? What are you good at? What do others call out in you? What breaks your heart?

Jesus is asking you to come, follow, go; to surrender in order to find; to let him repurpose your skills for the Kingdom; to believe the Spirit of the Lord has anointed you and sent you to bring good news, freedom, recovery, liberation, forgiveness, and healing to the world.

Questions for Reflection and Discussion

1. What does it mean to you to live a claimed, commissioned, and called life?

2. What brings you to life? How can you do more of it?

3. What do you know and love? What are you good at? How might God use your responses for Kingdom purposes?

4. What do others call out in you?

5. What breaks your heart?

CHAPTER

4

Journeying Together

Joining with Others
for Lasting Impact

SUSAN ROBB

CHAPTER 4

Journeying Together

Joining with Others for Lasting Impact

SUSAN ROBB

He also gave Hathach a copy of the law made public in Susa concerning the Jews' destruction so that Hathach could show it to Esther and report it to her. Through him Mordecai ordered her to go to the king to seek his kindness and his help for her people. Hathach came back and told Esther what Mordecai had said.

In reply Esther ordered Hathach to tell Mordecai: "All the king's officials and the people in his provinces know that there's a single law in a case like this. Any man or woman who comes to the king in the inner courtyard without being called is to be put to death. Only the person to whom the king holds out the gold scepter may live. In my case, I haven't been called to come to the king for the past thirty days."

When they told Mordecai Esther's words, he had them respond to Esther: "Don't think for one minute that, unlike all the other Jews, you'll come out of this alive simply because you are in the palace. In fact, if you don't speak up at this very important time, relief and rescue will appear for the Jews from another place, but you and your family will die. But who knows? Maybe it was for a moment like this that you came to be part of the royal family."

Esther sent back this word to Mordecai: "Go, gather all the Jews who are in Susa and tell them to give up eating to help me be brave. They aren't to eat or drink anything for three whole days, and I myself will do the same, along with my female servants. Then, even though it's against the law, I will go to the king; and if I am to die, then die I will."

Esther 4: 8-16

I don't know about you, but I've always been just a little envious of people who, at least on the outside, have projected a clear, singular certainty of their call and purpose in life since a young age. They are the ones who relentlessly pursued their one dream or passion, attained it, and continued living out their lives completely content with the one path they have chosen. It seems as if they came prewired for one purpose or vocation and set off flying solo, doggedly working on their own, to pursue it.

My life (especially my various callings in life) hasn't been as straightforward or as singular as theirs, and my guess is that yours hasn't been either. Even those who appear to be living with a singular purpose in mind probably took a more circuitous path than we realize and, rather than flying solo, probably had the encouragement, guidance, and support of more people than we could ever know. In the past, I have been deeply intentional about discerning and pursuing the call to be a high school teacher, wife, mother, United Methodist minister, and author. Some of those calls were obvious and others were not (at least to me).

Many of our passions, or callings, in life seem to bubble up from deep within. They truly are a part of how we are wired—how God created us. When I was a little girl, I would line my dolls and stuffed animals up on the sofa, prop a chalk board in a chair in front of them, and begin to teach them the alphabet and math problems. Teaching was in my blood. So it came as no surprise to many people when I decided to major in education in college.

At the age of four, after a field trip to the symphony, our son declared, "When I grow up, I'm going to play the violin!" No matter how much we tried to convince him that the piano would be more fun (we owned a piano, not a violin), he persisted. At age six, after two years of cajoling and battling, we finally caved in and bought him a cute little quarter-sized violin. He fell in love with the instrument from day one and played in orchestras from the time he was in elementary school all the way through college. It seemed as if the instrument chose the child and not the other way around. Only later did I remember that my maternal grandfather had the gift of being able to play the "fiddle" by ear and was always in demand at local square dances. Was it coincidence that my son fell in love with the same instrument his great-grandfather (whom he had never met) played? Maybe, or maybe not. But there was something about the violin that called his name, and he was passionate about it.

In the movie *Chariots of Fire*, there is a scene where the main character, Eric Liddell, is being reprimanded by his sister for wanting to pursue his dream of becoming an Olympic runner because it would require him to postpone their crucial missionary work. Eric responds to her disapproval by saying, "I believe God made me for a purpose...but he also made me fast. And when I run, I feel his pleasure."[1] Liddell didn't abandon one call to pursue another. He followed both callings, both passions, in an order that made sense. He broke standing Olympic records, becoming a medalist in the 1924 Summer Olympics. Afterwards, he and his sister traveled on to China to fulfill their purpose and passion as missionaries.

When we follow God's call in using our God-given gifts, the path of discernment seems easier, and we certainly feel God's pleasure. But sometimes, as with my call to be a minister, a thought or idea seems to come from out of the blue. We wonder if that seemingly crazy, dangerous, or impractical idea is truly God's, our own wild imagination, or someone else's misdirected fantasy. We need others to help us ascertain God's call and how best to pursue that call.

When we follow God's call in using our God-given gifts, the path of discernment seems easier.

Hearing God's Call Through Others

Many years ago, my husband and I sponsored a friend to attend a spiritual retreat called The Walk to Emmaus. As part of the retreat, we sponsors attended a prayer service for the attendees that culminated with Communion being served. Before the beginning of the service, the spiritual director of the retreat, whom I had never met, approached me and asked, "Would you mind helping serve Communion at the end of the service?" "Of course," I said. "I would love to help!" The spiritual director then instructed that we would be serving by intinction, "So, as each person comes forward, I will offer them a piece of bread and say, 'The body of Christ broken for you.' Then you will offer the cup saying, 'The blood of Christ given for you.'"

Incredibly honored to be chosen (although randomly) to participate in such a sacred moment, I approached this act of service with great reverence and enthusiastic awe. As I cupped the chalice in my hand, looking into the eyes of each participant as they dipped their bread into the cup, the words, "The blood of Christ given for you," became a holy mantra of sorts, repeated over, and over, and over again. And then something surreal happened. I sensed God saying to me, through a thought that was as clear as crystal, "This is what you're supposed to be doing."

But what, I wondered, does *this* mean? I pondered that question for a *very* long time. Does *this* mean I'm supposed to become more active in the church? Does *this* mean I'm supposed to enroll in seminary in order to become a more educated Sunday school teacher? Or could *this* possibly mean that God is calling me to ordained ministry?" All of the above seemed, in the least, to be impractical if not more than a little crazy. I had two children in diapers, and my husband and I were already very active leaders in the church. I loved my life as a stay-at-home mom and didn't have the time or the desire to have that life disrupted. "God," I wondered, "is this your idea, or just my crazy imagination?" I tried to ignore the thought that God was calling me to something new, but the words spoken so clearly in my mind during the Communion service kept nagging at me. They wouldn't leave me alone. The answers to all the questions above unfolded sometimes in quick bursts and sometimes more slowly, but they definitely weren't answered through my wrestling with them on my own. It took the voice of one person to confirm God's call and, subsequently, the prayers and voices of many in the community to help give guidance to that call.

Such is the story of Esther.

A Time Such as This

If you are unfamiliar with Esther's call story, or if it's been a while since you've read it, let me offer some background to the narrative that leads to her recognition of God's call in her life and her discerning the wisdom crucial to answering that call.

The Book of Esther is an etiology, a story that offers an explanation of how something came to be. Esther narrates the beginnings of the Jewish festival of Purim, the celebration of

God's salvation of the Jews from annihilation during the time of the Persian Empire. But the story also narrates Esther's call to discover and act on God's purpose for her life. The story is set, of course, in the Persian Empire in a province called Susa. Many Jews had been living there since their families had been dispersed from Judah generations before during the Babylonian exile. Two of those Jews, the story's main characters, are Mordecai, who serves in the king's court, and his younger cousin, Esther. Esther is Mordecai's charge. He has lovingly raised Esther as his own child since the death of her parents many years before.

Esther is written in a satirical, almost comedic, tongue-in-cheek style, using overblown and sometimes buffoonish characters (like the king and his advisors) to grapple with a grave subject: genocide.

Mordecai and Esther, like the multitude of other Jews living in Persia, have no memory of Judah and Jerusalem. They have largely assimilated into the Persian culture. After all, Persia is their home. Even so, as Jews, they are still considered by many to be foreigners in the only land they have ever known. Sound familiar? How many people dispersed from a plethora of countries have lived in America their entire lives and yet continue to endure the prejudices of others, being treated as foreigners in the only home they've ever known?

Through a twist of fate, the astoundingly beautiful Esther captures the attention and hearts of those in the king's palace (including the king!) and is selected to be queen after the king dismisses his first wife over a slight (and comical) snub. Although not evident in the beginning, racial tensions simmer under the surface of the story, and there are those (especially one of the king's advisors) who are eager to be rid of all the Jews in the kingdom. Wisely, Mordecai asks Esther to keep her Jewish heritage a secret from all who live behind the palace walls.

One of the king's advisors, Haman, who holds a grudge against Mordecai, and thus all of the Jews, approaches the king with a sinister, yet crafty, request: "A certain group of people...among the other peoples in all the provinces of your kingdom. Their laws are different from those of everyone else, and they refuse to obey the king's laws. There's no good reason for the king to put up with them any longer. If the king wishes, let a written order be sent out to destroy them" (Esther 3:8-9). The king, often duped by his advisors, agrees to Haman's proposal without so much as an investigation to determine who these "people" are, or if the report of their lawlessness is true (it isn't).

The decree is summarily issued to "destroy, to kill, and to annihilate all the Jews" on a prescribed future date, throwing the entire kingdom (including Mordecai) into confusion. As he sits in sackcloth and ashes, mourning the fate of his people, Mordecai sends word of the decree through a messenger to Esther, who sits oblivious behind the protection of the palace walls. Upon hearing the horrifying news, Esther too is deeply concerned, but even more so when Mordecai suggests in his message that she go to the king, expose her identity as a Jew, and beg him to save her and her people.

Esther likes her life behind the palace walls. She likes being queen. She likes having attendants and all the comforts the title of queen brings with it. She loves the king, and she thinks he probably still loves her, but she also knows how fickle he can be. Look what happened to the last queen! She doesn't want to rock the lovely boat she's living in. Esther has no desire to have her comfortable life disrupted. And besides, she hasn't been called before the king in over thirty days! Esther is well aware that if you go before the king unsummoned, it could cost you your life. Only if he extends his royal scepter to you, may your life be spared. So Esther, in essence, responds to Mordecai's plea by saying, "No thank you! I think I'll continue to sit firmly here and take my chances."

Did I mention that there is no mention of God anywhere in the Book of Esther? There isn't. However, God's presence, intervention, guidance, and call are palpable on every page of this beloved book. Through a series of "coincidences," we are led to assume that God is working, undetected, behind the scenes. We don't know exactly why God is never mentioned. Perhaps the author is trying to make the point that God speaks to us through nudges and through others and that God depends on the action and agency of God's people to bring about God's purposes in the world. If we think that God isn't active in the world, doesn't speak to us anymore, or doesn't need our voices, hands, and feet to bring about God's purposes in the world, perhaps we should be more attentive and listen more carefully to others.

When Esther dismisses Mordecai's insistence that she go to the king because it would be too dangerous, she finally hears her call clearly through his voice,

> *"Don't think for one minute that, unlike all the other Jews, you'll come out of this alive simply because you are in the palace. In fact, if you don't speak up at this very important time, relief and rescue will appear for the Jews from another place, but you and your family will die. But who knows? Maybe it was for a moment like this that you came to be part of the royal family."*
>
> *Esther 4:12-14*

The implication is that if Esther says "no" to her call, God will use someone else to bring deliverance to the Jews, but she will have missed the opportunity and perish besides. Perhaps she became queen, Mordecai's words intimate, not only to please the king or to have a life filled with luxuries but also for a deeper purpose. Perhaps she came to royal dignity in order to leverage her royal influence "for a moment like this."

Mordecai's words hit Esther with such force that there was no denying her call and what she must do to answer that call. But how should she approach this life-threatening endeavor? It will take more wisdom than her young mind possesses to navigate convincing the king to see her and to save all the Jews in his kingdom, all while protecting her own life. Esther is wise enough to know that she needs the help of the entire community, so she announces her own decree to Mordecai:

> *"Go, gather all the Jews who are in Susa and tell them to give up eating to help me be brave. They aren't to eat or*

If we think that God isn't active in the world, doesn't speak to us anymore, or doesn't need our voices, hands, and feet to bring about God's purposes in the world, perhaps we should be more attentive and listen more carefully to others.

drink anything for three whole days, and I myself will do
the same, along with my female servants. Then, even though
it's against the law, I will go to the king; and if I am to die,
then die I will."

Esther 4:15-16

I love that this young woman, who has always been obedient to everyone else's orders and demands, especially Mordecai's, is now the one taking charge, but with great confidence tempered with humility.

After years of wrestling with the notion that God might be calling me to seminary, of trying to figure things out on my own, I finally prayed, "God, I don't know if this is your idea or just my crazy, right-brained imagination, but if this is what you want for me, then I pray that you would let it come through Ike." I had never shared the Emmaus experience with my husband, Ike, because I couldn't make sense of it. Immediately I felt complete relief, as if I was off the hook. I was beyond certain that my husband would never dream of my becoming a preacher. I could stop fretting about this.

But God has a great sense of humor. That very afternoon, after I had prayed, our son's kindergarten soccer team and all their parents attended an end-of-the-year celebration at everyone's favorite hamburger joint. Our family entered the line, received our hamburgers, and took a seat in a large booth. Another family approached our table, and the mother of another young boy on the team asked, "May we sit with you?" Within minutes of settling in at the table, she enthusiastically exclaimed, "Guess what I've done? I just finished my first semester at Perkins School of Theology!" She then continued to regale us with stories of how incredible the course work and the professors were and how much she loved being there. Immediately, Ike turned to me and asked, "You would enjoy doing that, wouldn't you?" Shocked, I offered a slight nod and said, "Yeah…maybe." But I thought to myself, "That was a total fluke! Right?"

The next evening, while Ike and I were having dinner with one of his clients and his wife, our conversation turned to theology. Later during dinner, I leaned toward the client's wife to engage her in conversation and overheard Ike saying to his client, "You just wait. Someday Susan is going to go to seminary." Those words, while not directed at me, hit me with force. Immediately I thought, "Whoa! This is not a fluke!"

As Ike and I sat across from each other the next night over dinner, alone, I caught his gaze and said, "There's something I need to talk with you about." With our eyes still locked, he nodded and said only these words, "I know…I know." Sometimes, like Esther, we think we may have heard God's voice, but the call seems preposterous, or dangerous, or like the timing is just not right, so we need the clarity and encouragement—the voice—of someone else to recognize it. Just like Samuel needed Eli, and Esther needed Mordecai, I needed Ike's voice to confirm that this call was not crazy or part of an imagination gone wild, but God's call.

I've met many Mordecais (and Elis) in my life, and my guess is that you have as well. My high school English teacher offered clarity in my call to pursue a degree in education. A high school dance instructor encouraged me to utilize my passion in dance to work with high school girls. Friends and other ministers at the church helped me discern God's call to serve in various capacities and roles within the church, and to become an author. My guess is that you have had similar instances that helped guide you in your call(s) in life. What about now? Where might God be using others to speak to you today as you listen for God's voice? Who are the mentors, companions, or friends who can help guide you in fulfilling God's call?

Once we, like Esther, are certain of our call, we then need those in the community around us to help us determine our path forward. We sometimes hear people speak of discovering their purpose in life and following it through faith, as if it is an individual sport. We often act as if somehow faith is totally a matter of personal growth, personal fulfillment, personal salvation, but that's not the case at all. During my years in ministry, it became apparent that the Christian life is not best lived out as an individual sport but practiced much like a team sport.

Esther senses this intuitively.

Hearing God's Call Through Community— Listening and Living Together

Now that Esther is certain of her call, she knows she can no longer hide behind the palace's walls of security and

Christian life is not best lived out as an individual sport but practiced much like a team sport.

comfort. She must speak up. For the first time in her life, the young, meek, obedient Esther begins acting with confidence. With rapid fire conviction, she orders Mordecai to gather all of the Jews he can find to hold a fast on her behalf. She will do the same with her maids.

Remember, God isn't mentioned in the Book of Esther, but throughout the Old Testament fasting is normally coupled with wearing sackcloth, and is almost always paired with prayer. So when Esther calls for a fast on her behalf, it may also signify, for those who fear to invoke the name of God, that they should also pray for her. Esther needs time to prepare a plan. She needs courage, she needs the support of everyone around her to help her hold on to that courage, and more importantly, Esther needs the divine wisdom of God to discern the best way to approach this fickle king. Calling everyone to fast (and, by implication, to pray) is a good start.

My guess is that in those three days of fasting (and praying), those who were surrounding Esther may have said, "Have you thought about doing this?" "May I share an idea I've had with you?" Fasting and praying offer us time to listen—to our inner thoughts and convictions, to the advice and wisdom of others, and to the voice of God.

After three days, Esther knows not only what she must do (go to the king), but more importantly, *how* she must do it. Shored up by her community and with God's wisdom, Esther decides to adorn herself in all of her queenly splendor, royal robes and all. She wants to remind the king of who she is—*his* Queen. As she nervously approaches the throne room, the doors are flung open, and she confidently catches the gaze of the man across the room whose heart, at least in the beginning, belonged to her. To Esther's relief (and ours), the king extends his golden scepter in her direction and asks what he can do for her. Instead of throwing herself at his feet sobbing and begging for help as we might expect, Esther wisely does something different. She invites him to a banquet that very day. At the end of their lovely time together, eating dinner, drinking wine, laughing, and getting reacquainted, the king asks again what her request of him might be. "If I please the king, and if the king wishes to grant my wish and my desire, I'd like the king and Haman to come to another feast that I will prepare for them. Tomorrow I will answer the king's questions" (Esther 5:8). Esther wants to ensure that the king remembers his love for her and that their relationship is firmly sealed before she springs any bad news on him.

Esther's time spent with the community supporting her through fasting (and prayer) indeed brought her the wisdom she needed to take the first steps in her call journey. Her community quietly affirmed that they had confidence in her call to go before the king on their behalf. If you remember the story of Samuel from chapter 1, it was the Israelite community that affirmed their support of Samuel's call to be a prophet: "All Israel from Dan to Beer-sheba knew that Samuel was trustworthy as the LORD's prophet" (I Samuel 3:20). They recognized the gifts Samuel possessed for ministering to and leading them, gifts that would one day shape them into the people God called them to be. Esther's community does the same through their joint fasting (and prayer).

I love the words of Karl Barth, "To clasp hands in prayer is the beginning of an uprising against the disorder of the world." That was certainly true for Esther and her community, and it's true for us too. Through communal prayer we can best hear from God through our own thoughts and the thoughts of others informed by the Holy Spirit. When we clasp hands together in prayer, we are given the wisdom and courage we need to do work that seems impossible.

Listening to those around us is important. In the church, when a person has an inward call to ministry or service, it is outwardly affirmed by other ministers in the church, or congregants, who recognize a person's gifts for ministry (lay or ordained). I serve on a board that interviews candidates for ordained ministry. After someone tells us why they feel called to ministry, we then ask, "How have those in your church and community affirmed that call in you and your gifts for ministry?" They may offer that they are often asked to teach Bible studies or Sunday morning classes, or act as a lay preacher. They may say that several people have told them they think that they should go to seminary or be a preacher. Our inward call should always be affirmed and guided by the community of faith.

This is the case not just with ministry, but with a variety of professions. When I was a little girl, and beyond, I dreamt of being a dancer on Broadway. While I was a very good dancer, even throughout my college years, and performed in local theatre productions, auditions for a touring Broadway musical in Dallas did not affirm a call to Broadway! Becoming a teacher, doctor, nurse, lawyer, accountant, or minister (just to name a few) requires that one not only possess an internal passion or call, but that call must also be affirmed by others through entry exams, adequate grades, vocational and professional boards, or words of affirmation. Listen carefully to others' appreciation of your gifts, of the ways in which you make them feel affirmed or cared for. Listen to their needs and hopes for the future. Their words may just be the seeds, affirmation, or guidance of God's call in your life.

Living Out Our Call with Community

After two days of wining and dining, and luxuriating in each other's company, the king asks Esther a third time, "What is your petition, Queen Esther?" It is now time for Esther to open the king's eyes to the truth of the sinister plot to which he has blindly been a party, and to solicit his help in saving her and her people.

Be careful who you hate, it might be someone you love. That saying is one a friend of mine is fond of sharing. Unwittingly, the king has been duped into hating someone he loves dearly: his queen, Esther. The king's question, "What is your petition, Queen Esther?" prompts her response:

> *"Give me my life—that's my wish—and the lives of my people too.... We have been sold—I and my people—to be wiped*

Our inward call should always be affirmed and guided by the community of faith.

out, killed, and destroyed. If we simply had been sold as male and female slaves, I would have said nothing. But no enemy can compensate the king for this kind of damage."

Esther 7:3b-4

An awkward and energized conversation ensues. Once the king realizes Haman has duped him into hating an innocent people and issuing a decree that would end their lives and that of his very own wife, he sends Haman to the gallows. While the king legally can't revoke a decree he has made, he does give permission to Esther and Mordecai to devise an alternate plan. They are allowed to issue another decree in the king's name permitting the Jews throughout the kingdom to defend themselves by killing anyone who tries to kill them. Esther and Mordecai's decree inspires all in the Jewish community to work together to thwart the evil plans of those who would seek their destruction.

The wisdom Esther gleans from the fasting (and prayers) of the community helps her approach the king in a way that reinforces his love and favor. One well-timed conversation leads to another and ultimately leads to Esther and Mordecai inspiring the community to work together for their salvation. Their praying together and working together changes the trajectory of all of their lives and changes the trajectory of a nation. Together, through God's grace, they accomplish what they never could have done alone.

God means for us to live out our call *in* community, *with* the community of faith. It is good for us to remember that in the Book of Acts, the church is born when the Holy

Spirit lands not on one sole person who works tirelessly to bring about the kingdom of God, but rather on the entire community of faith gathered together, that they might *all* witness to the love and power of God *together* (Acts 2).

Being part of a group, working together for a common purpose, whether that is a group of three (like Esther, the king, and Mordecai), or twelve, or twelve hundred, galvanizes those gathered to accomplish far more than one person acting alone. No doubt, you've witnessed this in your own community and church. Together you may serve not one, but two hundred meals for Meals on Wheels, you can build an entire house for Habitat for Humanity, you can support an orphanage rather than one child. The list is endless as to what you can do together with the Holy Spirit's power and guidance, and when you do, my guess is that you feel God's pleasure. Where and how might God be calling you to partner with others to bring your gifts and passions together for greater impact?

Several years ago, a group of women leaving a worship service on a Sunday morning spied a young woman standing in the parking lot of the church, clutching a few dollars in her hand and sobbing. The women approached this young woman, asked what was wrong and if they could help her in some way. She disclosed that she had been attending their church for some weeks, and she said, "For the first time in my life, I've heard that God loves me, and I've come to know this is true. I wanted to place this money in the offering plate today—to give something back to God—but I couldn't. It's dirty money." The young woman went on to explain that she worked in an exotic dance club and had been trafficked into the sex industry at a very young age by a family member. She desperately wanted to get out of the life she was living, but she didn't know how. It was the only life (and profession) she had ever known. "I don't know what else I can do," she cried. This compassionate group of church women spent the next year setting aside their own agendas in order to serve one purpose: to help this young woman find a new way of life. They spent the next year surrounding her in love, offering her financial assistance so she could get her GED, find an apartment, and obtain meaningful employment. After her life turned around and she discovered her worth as a child of God, many of her friends came to these same women for help as well. Amy's Friends was born and is now called New Friends New Life. I served on the advisory board of New Friends New Life for many years, and it became one of the ministries supported by our church. This agency now offers hope to more than 1,200 formerly trafficked teens, women, and their children each year—all due to a group of women who heard and followed God's call to help one person, then another, and another. Soon their entire church community followed them in that call. Together they achieved more to bring about the kingdom of God on earth as it is in heaven than they could have ever done on their own.

You can too. You, like Esther and the women I just mentioned, are born "for a moment like this." You can use your gifts and leverage your influence for the betterment of those around you. Listen, like Esther (and Samuel), to the

You use your gifts and leverage your influence for the betterment of those around you.

voice of God in your life through the voice of others. Follow your many calls (both your "big-C" and "little-c" callings) through the guidance of the community of Christ. As you do, may you live out your call within your community of faith. When you do, you will be amazed at what God can do through your saying "yes" to the call placed on your life. Your life will never be the same, and neither will the lives of those around you.

Questions for Reflection and Discussion

1. Who has been a "Mordecai" in your life?

2. In your various roles, what gifts and what kinds of influence do you have in others' lives? How are you currently using your gifts and influence?

3. How have you worked in conjunction with the community to offer God's grace and love and/or bring needed change?

4. Is there something new you sense God is calling you to? How can you now better discern that call?

Ideas for
Journaling

Journaling can be a helpful way to clarity and insight, opening yourself to God's voice through active reflection. The following pages contain questions and prompts based on the insights in this book to help you listen for God's voice. Set aside time each day (fifteen to twenty minutes) to write in a journal or notebook using these questions and prompts as a guide.

Voices

What voices do you hear each day? each week? each month? List all the voices you can think of—these can be family members, friends, colleagues, authors, TV or internet personalities, advertisements, songs, and so forth.

How would you recognize if God were speaking to you through one of these voices?

The Sound of God's Voice

What does God's voice "sound like" to you? How has God spoken to you in the past, or how do you expect God to speak?

What experiences have given you an opportunity to learn what God's voice sounds like?

What opportunities have you had to "practice" listening to God?

Ideas for Journaling

What are some ways, right now, that you can practice listening and learning what God's voice sounds like in your life?

Obstacles

Have you ever found it difficult to hear God's voice because you were disobeying God? How would making a change allow you to open yourself more fully to God's voice?

Have you ever found it difficult to hear God because other voices were too loud or distracting?

What might God be trying to tell you that you don't want to hear? How can you listen for God's voice with openness and a willingness to hear even hard things?

What is something God might be calling you to say or do that might be difficult? Is there a calling or nudging in your life that seems challenging or risky?

Uncertainty

Where are you experiencing uncertainty about the future right now?

What do you wish you could know in advance?

What would it mean for you to take things one day, one step, at a time? What is the next faithful step God is calling you to take as you consider this uncertain future?

Practical Steps

Living one day at a time. Scripture. Others. Silence. Which of these practical steps resonates most with you?

Which of them do you find hardest to practice?

How can you open yourself more fully to one or more of these steps in the days and weeks ahead?

Choose one of the practical steps discussed in this book and write about it. What would it mean for you to practice this step more intentionally? What do you hope to hear from God as you open yourself in this way?

God's Calling

Are you feeling the Spirit prompting you in any way right now? What do you feel God may be calling you to do?

How do you feel about this? What questions or hesitations do you have? What excites you about it?

Draw a large letter *C* on a page of your journal or notebook. Think back through your life and recall times when the Holy Spirit has prompted you to do something. Identify as many instances as you can, and write them in short words and phrases around the large letter *C*.

Look for connections that emerge from these past leadings of the Holy Spirit. Draw lines connecting events that are similar or seem otherwise related.

Do any patterns or themes come to the surface?

Bringing You to Life

What brings you to life? When do you feel most alive and full of purpose and joy?

What does it feel like when you are doing it? Why do you experience such joy and fulfillment through this thing?

Is the answer to this question clear, or does it seem hard to identify one specific thing?

Something New

Consider whether God might be leading you to try something new. Have you felt curious or excited about something you've never done before? What is this?

What practical steps would you need to take in order to try this new thing?

Is there something new you sense God is calling you to do or pursue?

What thoughts and feelings do you have about it? What questions and hesitations do you have?

What hopes and expectations do you have in regard to this new thing?

Who Is Your Mordecai?

Write the names of your mentors and other influential people in your life. As you write each name, offer a simple, silent prayer of thanks for that person.

How did these people serve as Mordecai for you? How did they help you gain clarity when considering a big decision or some other aspect of God's call?

Where and how might God be using others to speak to you now as you listen for God's voice?

Helping Others Discern God's Voice

List the people in your life whom you influence—children or family members, students, colleagues, and so forth. What others look to you for advice or guidance? As you write their names, say a prayer of thanks for each person and invite God to use you to speak to them.

What might this person need to hear from God? How do you know? What questions or uncertainties have they expressed to you?

How can you serve as a Mordecai for this person? What opportunities do you have to give them counsel or advice in a way that they will hear and appreciate?

What's Next?

Has the Holy Spirit brought you any clarity or direction or sense of conviction through this book?

What do you sense God wants you to do next? Write down any next steps that seem like the right path forward. Be as specific as possible. (You may see many next steps, or only one or two.)

What would it mean for you to take this next step? What would you have to risk? What opportunities would it open up for you? What doors would it close?

Ideas for Journaling

What would it mean if you choose not to take this step?

Who else would be involved if you take this step?

What would they have to do or give up? What would they gain?

How do you need their support and encouragement?

Bible Verses
to Read
in Times
of Trouble

Consider these Bible verses when you are:

FEARFUL

Deuteronomy 31:8
Isaiah 43:1
1 John 4:18
2 Timothy 1:7

CONCERNED ABOUT DEATH

Psalm 23:4
Isaiah 25:8
John 11:26
Romans 8:38-39

TRYING TO BE A GOOD PARENT

Deuteronomy 6:6-7
Proverbs 22:6
Ephesians 6:4
3 John 1:4

WORRIED ABOUT THE FUTURE

Romans 15:13
Romans 8:28
Philippians 4:7
1 Peter 5:7

CONCERNED ABOUT THE STATE OF THE WORLD

Isaiah 54:10
Matthew 5:14-16
John 16:33
Galatians 6:9

GRIEVING THE LOSS OF A LOVED ONE

Psalm 30:5
Psalm 34:8
Matthew 5:4
Revelation 21:4

FEELING HELPLESS

Psalm 18:2
Isaiah 12:2
Matthew 19:26
Philippians 4:13

DEALING WITH ANGER

Proverbs 15:1
Colossians 3:8
Ephesians 4:26
James 1:19-20

PRAYING FOR SOMEONE ELSE

Matthew 18:19
James 5:13-16
Romans 8:26-27
Hebrews 4:16

CONCERNED ABOUT HEALTH

Psalm 6:2
Jeremiah 17:14
Jeremiah 33:6
James 5:13-15

STRUGGLING TO FORGIVE

Matthew 18:21-22
Mark 11:25
Ephesians 4:31-32
Colossians 3:13

CONCERNED ABOUT THE PLANET

Leviticus 25:23-24
Psalm 24:1
Psalm 89:11
Isaiah 24:4-6

TRYING TO KNOW GOD'S WILL

1 Kings 19:11-13
Psalm 37:4-5
Proverbs 3:5-6
Romans 12:1-2

REPAIRING A BROKEN RELATIONSHIP

James 5:16
Luke 6:27
Proverbs 10:12
Romans 12:17

GIVING THANKS TO GOD

Psalm 9:1
Hebrews 12:28
1 Thessalonians 5:16-18
James 1:17

FEELING TOO BUSY AND OVERWHELMED

Matthew 11:28-29
Psalm 46:10
Proverbs 23:4
1 Corinthians 10:31

FEELING DEPRESSED

Psalm 4:8
Psalm 143:8
Isaiah 40:31
Isaiah 41:10

SEEKING CONTENTMENT

Proverbs 14:30
Proverbs 19:23
Philippians 4:11-13
1 Timothy 6:6-12

TRYING TO MAKE A CAREER DECISION

Proverbs 3:5-6
Proverbs 16:3
Colossians 3:23
Jeremiah 29:11

FEELING GUILT OR SHAME

Psalm 103:12
Isaiah 1:18
2 Corinthians 5:17
1 John 1:9-10

DESIRING TO BE MORE FAITHFUL TO GOD

Deuteronomy 5:33
Mark 8:34
James 2:17
1 Peter 2:21

NOTES

Chapter 2

1 William McCaskill, *What We Owe the Future* (Basic Books, 2022), 223-224.

2 Philip Yancey, *Disappointment with God: Three Questions No One Asks Aloud* (Zondervan, 2015), 224.

3 Queen Elizabeth II, quoted in Dudley Delffs, "Died: Queen Elizabeth II, British Monarch Who Put Her Trust in God," *Christianity Today*, September 8, 2022. https://www.christianitytoday.com/news/2022/september/obit-queen-elizabeth-ii-personal-faith-christian-bible.html

4 Queen Elizabeth II, Christmas Broadcast 2002. Accessed April 17, 2023. https://www.royal.uk/christmas-broadcast-2002

5 Parker J. Palmer, "The Clearness Committee: A Communal Approach To Discernment," Center for Courage and Renewal. Accessed April 17, 2023. https://couragerenewal.org/library/the-clearness-committee-a-communal-approach-to-discernment/

6 Edgar Allan Poe, "An Opinion on Dreams," *Burton's Gentleman's Magazine*, August 1839. Accessed April 18, 2023. https://www.eapoe.org/works/rejected/opindrms.htm

7 Sander van der Linden, "The Science Behind Dreaming," *Scientific American*, July 26, 2011. Accessed April 18, 2023.https://www.scientificamerican.com/article/the-science-behind-dreaming

8 Janine MacLachlan, "Want to Be More Creative? Be Like Edison and Take a Nap," *Forbes*, January 9, 2022. Accessed April 18, 2023. https://www.forbes.com/sites/janinemaclachlan/2022/01/09/want-to-be-more-creative-be-like-edison-and-take-a-nap

Chapter 4

1 "God made me for a purpose" scene with brother and sister Eric Liddell and Jennie Liddell, *Chariots of Fire*, directed by Hugh Hudson (1981; Twentieth Century Fox).

**Watch videos
based on
*On Purpose:
Finding God's Voice
in Your Passion*
through
Amplify Media.**

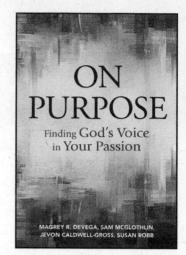

Amplify Media is a multimedia platform that delivers high quality, searchable content with an emphasis on Wesleyan perspectives for churchwide, group, or individual use on any device at any time. In a world of sometimes overwhelming choices, Amplify gives church leaders and congregants media capabilities that are contemporary, relevant, effective and, most importantly, affordable and sustainable.

With *Amplify Media* church leaders can:

- Provide a reliable source of Christian content through a Wesleyan lens for teaching, training, and inspiration in a customizable library
- Deliver their own preaching and worship content in a way the congregation knows and appreciates
- Build the church's capacity to innovate with engaging content and accessible technology
- Equip the congregation to better understand the Bible and its application
- Deepen discipleship beyond the church walls

**Ask your group leader or pastor about Amplify Media
and sign up today at www.AmplifyMedia.com.**